HOW TO BE HOLY

PETER J. KREEFT

HOW TO BE HOLY

First Steps in Becoming a Saint

A Festooning of
Abandonment to Divine Providence

IGNATIUS PRESS   SAN FRANCISCO

Cover design by
www.AmpersandMiami.com

© 2016 by Ignatius Press, San Francisco
All rights reserved
ISBN 978-1-62164-102-5
Library of Congress Control Number 2015953761
Printed in the United States of America ∞

Dedicated to Mom (John 19:27)

Contents

1. Ten Reasons to Read This Book 9

2. A Radically Life-Changing Idea 19

3. Why This Idea Is Not As Ridiculous As It Seems 24

4. An Irrefutable Logical Proof of Its Truth 28

5. How This Truth Changes Your Life 33

6. God as Your Guru 36

7. How Divine Providence Does
   What Seems Impossible 43

8. Faith and Reason: Can We Believe It
   if We Don't Understand It? 46

9. Why Surrender Does Not Squash Individuality 50

10. Where to Find God:
    The Practice of the Presence of God 55

11. Overcoming Deism and the Absentee God . . . 61

12. The Epistemology of Holiness 67

13. Little Things 74

14. Holiness Is Easy 79

15. Methods 83

16. Faith, Hope, and Love Are Only One Thing . . 86

17. Unselfconsciousness 90

18. "Love Is All You Need" 93

19. Love and Sex 96

20. When to Find God:
    "The Sacrament of the Present Moment" . . . 98

21. The Future 104

22. Peace 108

23. Failures 110

24. Suffering 115

25. Objection: I Can't Be a Saint 120

26. Duties 123

27. Activity and Receptivity 125

28. Spiritual Warfare 128

29. Grace 131

30. Detachment 134

31. Creation 140

32. God and You Only? 142

33. Praying while Working 144

34. Gratitude 146

35. "Progressive" or "Conservative"? 150

Appendix 1: A Meditation on the Relationship
    between *Being* and God's Will 153
Appendix 2: A Dialogue between Stupid and Sensible
    (the Two Parts of My Soul) 159

I

Ten Reasons to Read This Book

The cover of this book is a joke. You're going to read *How to Be Holy* by whom? Mother Teresa? Saint John Paul II? Saint Francis of Assisi? No, by Peter Kreeft. That's like reading *How to Be Honest* by Pinocchio.

If you want to know how to be a sailor, do you read a book by a sailor or by a landlubber? If you want to know how to be an astronaut, do you read a book by a successful astronaut or by a wannabe astronaut? So if you want to read a book about how to be a saint, do you read a book by a saint or by an absent-minded philosophy professor?

If you choose the second, I have a time share in Florida that I'd like to sell you.

So why read this book?

I have ten answers.

Reason No. 1

One is that my very failure to practice what I preach is what you need if you, like me, are a beginner. In my own field, philosophy, I know that "experts" are often the last people to trust. Brilliant philosophers are often quite insane. Genius and insanity are often closely connected.

But the saints are not insane; in fact, they are the only truly sane people in the world because they are living in reality, in real reality, in ultimate reality, in God's reality. Despite what the Supreme Court says, it is the Supreme Being, not the Supreme Court, who invents and defines reality.

Even when the experts are not insane, they are sometimes not the best people for beginners to learn from at first. This is true in almost any field. Beginners in chess are usually better taught at first by other beginners than by grandmasters. For when the teachers are beginners, the teachers and students are together; they experience the same failures. This book is not a great chef serving up a gourmet dinner; it is one desperately poor bum telling another where there's free food.

Reason No. 2

My second answer is that this is all I have to give you. But even a little answer to a great question is more precious than a great answer to a little question. For instance, a small change of diet or exercise that gives you a little more health and alertness and longevity is more important than a complete and perfect repair of your bathroom. The merit of this book is in the topic more than in my treatment of it. How to be holy, how to be a saint, is the most important topic I have ever written about. It's the whole meaning of life, the "one thing necessary". So even if I can help only one person become a little holier, that's more important than helping a million people become a lot more "successful" at anything else. Because nothing else is eternal. "You can't take it with you" applies to everything except yourself.

Reason No. 3

Third, and most important of all, the wisdom in this book is not from me. It's from God and His saints. I just pass it on.

In this field, I am only a translator, not an original author. I am not any kind of "expert". The only experts in this field are the saints. And I'm about as close to being a saint as I am to being a salamander.

Why, then, read my book? Because this book is not about my ideas, it's about the ideas of thousands of saints throughout history. In particular, it's my "festooning" (like decorating a Christmas tree) of the main points of one of the simplest and most practical of all classics of spiritual direction, de Caussade's *Abandonment to Divine Providence*.[1]

Reason No. 4

So you should read this book if you are a rank beginner because that's who I wrote it for. That's why it's so simple. I wrote this kind of book once before—an extended nonscholarly commentary on another very simple spiritual classic, Brother Lawrence's *The Practice of the Presence of God*, which I called *Prayer for Beginners*. I chose these

---

[1] All quotations from Jean-Pierre de Caussade's *Abandonment to Divine Providence* are taken from the translation by John Beevers (1975; Garden City, N.Y.: Image Books, 2014).

books to comment on because they were both simple. They are great little books for beginners.

I also wrote a much longer and more detailed book, *Practical Theology: Spiritual Direction from Saint Thomas Aquinas (How Your Mind Can Make You Holy)*, because Aquinas helped me a lot, not just intellectually, in my thinking, because he was a great philosopher and theologian, but also practically, in my walk with God, because he was a great saint; and I wanted to share with you the help I got from him. This book is about the same thing and written with the same motive, but it's short and simple and makes only one point instead of 350 of them, as the book on Aquinas did.

Reason No. 5

That brings up another reason for reading it: because it's a short book (both de Caussade's and mine), and short books are the most powerful, as lean meat is the most nourishing.

Reason No. 6

One of the reasons it's simple is because, like de Caussade and most of the saints, it sits light on methods.

For, after all, what is a method but a technology, that is, a repeatable, impersonal, and objective technique for causing some desired change through the least personal effort, like pressing a key or flipping a switch. Technology makes some part of life easier. But sanctity is not a part of life; it's the meaning and end of life; and it does not make life *easier*, only more unified and more joyful.

For sanctity is love, and love never makes life easier, only more unified and joyful. There is no technique for sanctity because there is no technique for love and sanctity is love.

But that's the whole point of life. The whole meaning of life is love: to love and let yourself be loved by God and your neighbor. Deep down, everybody knows that. The more important the question, the more certain and universal our knowledge of the answer is. And since that's the most important of all questions, that's the answer we all know with the most certainty, deep down.

And because love is the whole meaning of life, that's why "in the evening of our life we will be judged on our love" (Saint John of the Cross).

Love of course (and we all know this deep down, too, even though we often suppress it and rationalize its denial) is essentially not a feeling but a willing. That's why we are responsible for it: because it is in our power, as feelings are not. Feelings come to us, love comes from us. Feelings happen to us, we happen to love. Feelings do us, we do love.

Of course, feelings are good and natural allies of willing. Good feelings motivate good willings, and bad feelings motivate bad willings. Good feelings also follow good willings, and bad feelings (guilt, anger, resentment, impotence, fear, self-hatred) follow bad willings. That's why God gave us feelings: as motivators and as rewards (and punishments).

Reason No. 7

The simplicity of this book makes it universal. It's for everyone, no matter what their religion, because it's about the simple center and essence of all authentic religion.

Whenever I write the word "God", Christians will think of Jesus Christ. They will interpret all references to "God" as references to "the One Jesus called His (and our) Father".

Jews will read "God" as "the God of Abraham, Isaac, and Jacob, the God of the Law and the Prophets of Israel and of the Hebrew Scriptures". Good! That is exactly who Jesus meant by "God"!

Muslims will read "God" as "Allah, the One True God, the God of the Holy Qur'an". Fine: every one of the ninety-nine names of God in the Qur'an are also in the Jewish and Christian Scriptures.

Philosophical theists will read "God" as "the God Reason reveals". Fine. That is a pretty thick slice of the same God, the one and only God, who is also the God of religious revelation.

Hindus and some Buddhists and students of mysticism will read "God" as "the one infinitely beyond reason". Good. That is also true.

There are some specifically Christian and some specifically Catholic sentences in the book. The only way I could have kept them out would have been to put an unnatural lock on the door of my heart. But the main points of the book do not depend on them.

I am myself a totally convinced, "eat-everything-Mommy-puts-on-your-plate" Catholic Christian. This book is

Catholic as well as catholic (universal). If I were to choose a book written by a Muslim that I thought would have the most power to change my life, I would look for one by an "eat-everything-Mommy-puts-on-your-plate" Muslim, not a compromiser, a revisionist, a nice, generic, popular, Oprah-kind of Muslim. I'd look for a book you *wouldn't* find in airport bookstores. Everyone who has ever worked in interreligious dialogue knows that progress in this field is never made by generic, noncontroversial believers, but only by dialogue among those who are strongly convinced by and deeply in love with their own specific religions.

As a Roman Catholic Christian, I see God through Christ, and I see Christ through the teachings of the Church that I believe He founded, the apostolic Church that wrote and later canonized the New Testament. I also see Jesus' mother, Mary, as the ideal practitioner of the philosophy of this book, the ideal "abandoner" or "surrenderer", who said a simple, total Yes to God's will when He sent His angel to ask graciously for *permission* (!) for His Son to be born of her. She is also the one who summarized all the practical wisdom in the world in one simple sentence when she said to the wineless waiters at the wedding feast at Cana, "Do whatever he tells you" (Jn 2:5). She is thus the ideal Muslim (the word *means* "surrenderer"). She is also the ideal Jew. You cannot doubt that if you read her song, the "Magnificat" (Lk 2:68–79).

So when I write the word "God", I do not mean some lowest-common-denominator abstraction. I don't mean a particular concept of God because I don't mean *any* concept of God; I mean *God*, the God who transcends all concepts, the One God, the Real God, the Living Fire, the Unapproachable Light, the One Beyond All Words. All religions catch a glimpse of Him. None catch Him.

This book is written for twelve of the thirteen kinds of people in the world: (1) "Eat-everything-Mommy-puts-on-your-plate" Catholics like myself, (2) "Cafeteria Catholics", (3) Eastern Orthodox Christians, (4) Anglicans, (5) Biblical Protestants, (6) religious Jews, (7) Muslims, (8) theistic Hindus (who follow Ramanjua and bhakti yoga), (9) pantheistic Hindus (who follow Shankara and jnana yoga), (10) "Pure Land" "Other-Power" Buddhists, (11) generic theists who believe in AA's "Higher Power", (12) and even non-theistic, open-minded agnostics of all stripes who do not deliberately reject the idea of seeking the One infinitely perfect and undefinable God that all religions seek and who seek to live in His perfect will, who seek not just to be minimally "good" but to be saints, who seek not just to be "nice", but to be *holy*.

How holy? Jesus did not say "You know, It would be a good ideal for you to strive for if you tried to be just a little bit holier." He said, "You, therefore, must be perfect, as your heavenly Father is perfect" (Mt 5:48), because that is what God had said to His chosen people long ago: "Be holy, for I am holy" (Lev 11:44). "Perfect" does not mean "never made a mistake, never sinned". "Perfect" means "finished, completed".

Reason No. 8

And this brings us to my eighth reason for you to read a book about how to be holy. It is because holiness is the meaning of life. As Léon Bloy often said, "Life, in the end, has only one tragedy: not to have been a saint." Even the agnostic but open-minded and troubled atheist Albert Camus knew that. Dr. Rieux, his protagonist in *The Plague*, agonizes over the dilemma that (1) the meaning of life is to be a saint, and (2) you can't be a saint without God, but (3) there is no God.

Is being a saint really the whole meaning of life? Isn't getting to Heaven more important? Think this through. Ask yourself this question: Which is more important, justification or sanctification (in terms of Christian theology)? Being saved or being saintly?

Be honest with your answer. All you really want to do is get to Heaven, right? Being a saint—that's for the few, the fanatics, right? Getting into Heaven's stadium is more important than getting a box seat, right? Escaping Hell is more important than escaping mediocrity, right?

What's the word Jesus used to describe that attitude? It's in Revelation 3:16. It's a divinely inspired verb. It begins with a "v" and ends with a "t".

The angel said he was to be called "Jesus" ("Savior"), not because he would save his people from the *punishment* for their sins, but because he would save them from their *sins*. Not just the consequences of sins, not just punishment, not just damnation, not just Hell, but sins. What a mean, selfish, low notion it is to think of salvation as a free ticket to Heaven! It comes with a price. T. S. Eliot identifies the price nicely when he calls it "A condition of complete simplicity (Costing not less than everything)".

Love wants to give everything. If it doesn't, it's not really love.

Faith, which justifies us, is like a root. Hope, which expands us, is like a shoot. Love, which perfects us, is like a fruit. Which of these three equally necessary parts of the growing plant of our spiritual life is most important? Read 1 Corinthians 13 for the answer. The whole point of the root and the shoot is the fruit. The rest of the plant is *for* the fruit. The fruit is not an afterthought, an extra, an accident. Sanctification is to justification what babies are to sex.

Oh, sorry, I forgot. Modern sex education denies that. Babies are "accidents".

Reason No. 9

It's simple. Sanctity isn't rocket science. De Caussade says: "What is the secret of finding this treasure [holiness]? There isn't one. This treasure is everywhere. It is offered to us all the time and wherever we are" (p. 23). To be in search of it is like being a fish in search of the sea.

Reason No. 10

It will give you more than happiness; it will give you joy. Try it, you'll like it. Guaranteed.

2

A Radically Life-Changing Idea

That's quite a claim, that chapter title. What idea could that be?

"God is real" is a good candidate. If you put all the ideas that all human minds have ever come up with, from the moral law to $E = MC^2$, onto one side of a scale, and if you put just the one single idea of God onto the other side of the scale—the idea of a real Being infinitely perfect in every way—it would be like an elephant on one end of a seesaw and a hill of ants on the other.

But that's just an *idea*, even though it is the greatest of all ideas. The fact that the idea is *true*, that God is *real*, that God has the chutzpah to exist—that's even better.

But even that is not enough to be life-changing. He might exist "up there" but be like Rhett Butler in *Gone with the Wind* and not give a damn about us. Why should He? Why should God care about us? Why should He *love* us? Why should He love *you*, concretely and specifically and individually, with all your fears and follies and fantasies and faults—love you, not just in the sense that you love your cute, furry kitten or puppy, but love you with His whole will, willing always and only what is your best good—love you so much that He would literally do anything for you, even die for you. Wouldn't God have to be insane to do that?

And even that is not enough, because even if He wills your best good, He might not be able to accomplish it unless He is also all-powerful. And He might not know what is always best for you unless He is also all-knowing. Only a God who is (1) all-good, that is, who wills your best good and nothing but your best good, your true happiness, all the time, that is, is *omni-benevolent*; and also (2) *omni-potent*, or all-powerful, whose will is always infallibly done; and also (3) *omni-scient*, all-knowing and infallible, that is, only a God with these three personal attributes can change the meaning of your life.

In the Qur'an, the one true God (which is what "Allah" means) has one hundred names, ninety-nine of which are written and one of which cannot be written or spoken. This is strikingly similar to the Jewish Scriptures, in which God has many names but names Himself only once, to Moses from the Burning Bush, and there He does not call Himself anything; He just says "I am." (The word, JHWH in Hebrew, is so holy that no religious Jew will ever try to pronounce it.) He is more than all our names can name. But among His attributes, these three are the most necessary for us to know. Deny any one of the three, and the true God disappears and all the false gods, all the idols, reappear, from Zeus to Baal. A God who is not all-good, a God who has an evil side, a "dark side", like "The Force" in *Star Wars*, is not totally trustable, for he is half God and half devil. A God who is not all-powerful, a God who has weaknesses, is not totally trustable, even if He is good; He's just a big brother. And a God who is not all-wise, all-knowing, is not totally trustable because he is a God who makes mistakes about you and about what is best for you, like a well-intentioned but incompetent surgeon. A bad God, a weak God, or a stupid God is not God and cannot merit, demand, or receive that total trust, that "abandonment", which is the point of this book and the road to holiness. The three attributes of omnibenevolence, omnipotence, and omniscience are absolutely nonnegotiable, foundational, necessary.

Insofar as any religion grasps some truth about the real God (and I do not claim to know how much truth each religion does grasp, so please don't ask me), insofar as Allah or Brahman or Tao or the Buddha-Mind or Ahura Mazda or AA's "Higher Power" is *true*, none of them can be wicked, weak, or stupid.

To put the point in a single phrase, God is "that than which nothing greater can be conceived". That was Saint Anselm's definition for God. Or, rather, since the infinite God cannot be defined, that was his formula for distinguishing the true God from false gods.

Saint Anselm thought that formula was also a proof for God's existence, since he thought that real existence, compared to merely existing in man's thought, was a perfection, and since God had all perfections, He must therefore have real existence, too. I do not personally think that argument works logically (neither did Saint Thomas Aquinas), nor do I think it "defines" God, but I do think that Anselm's words do distinguish the true God from all false gods; for if x has any imperfection, x is not God. And though God has many more perfections than these three, He certainly has these three.

You are probably thinking: OK, fine, I believe all that, but so does half the world. That idea of an infinitely perfect God is quite familiar. How can it be "the most radical and life-changing idea that has ever entered a human mind"?

It is the practical *consequence* or corollary of this theological idea that is radically life-changing. And that consequence is my favorite verse in the Bible. It is also the hardest verse to believe, precisely because it seems literally too good to be true. The verse is Romans 8:28 (ESV):

For those who love God all things work together for good.

But how can believing this make us holy? Holiness is caused by how we love, with our hearts and wills, not by what we believe with our minds. (See Jas 2:19.) Furthermore, love is a human choice, an act that comes *from* us, from our own free will; but Romans 8:28 refers to the objective truth that all things are part of a perfect divine providence that come *to* us from God's will. I seem to be confusing will with intellect and human free choice with divine providential necessity.

The answer to this twofold objection is twofold.

First, intellect and will are both involved, and so are both faith and love. In fact, as chapter 16 will show, faith, hope, and love are all one thing, or aspects of one thing, the thing that de Caussade calls "abandonment". The faith that is a theological virtue is not just intellectual belief but personal trust. And the hope that is faith's arm extended into the future is not just optimism but confidence and trust in the God who always keeps His promises. And the love that is the fruit of this faith and hope is not just a subjective feeling but an objective reality; in fact, it is

God's own eternal life in our souls. These three theological (God-originated and God-targeted) virtues are as inseparable as the roots (faith), the shoots (hope), and the fruits (love) of a single plant.

The second answer is that the necessary source of the active choice to be holy is the vision of truth in Romans 8:28, the vision of the omnibenevolent, omniscient, and omnipotent God who is present in all events. In Heaven, because we see this God perfectly, it will be psychologically impossible for us to sin. Here on earth, both our vision and our holiness are imperfect. But insofar as we approach that face-to-face Heavenly vision by our faith, which sees "through a glass, darkly", we become increasingly holy.

This book shows how that works.

3

Why This Idea Is Not as Ridiculous as It Seems

You can see why Romans 8:28 sounds ridiculous in a world whose history is accurately summarized as "war briefly interrupted by peace, selfishness by charity, and pains by pleasures". It seems far worse than "too good to be true". It seems like the most ridiculously Pollyanna-ish romanticism and sentimentalism.

In Monty Python's satirical movie *The Life of Brian* (which some interpret as a satire on Christianity but I interpret as a satire on pop psychology's perversion of Christianity), Jesus is just a nice schlemiel who finds himself in the wrong place at the wrong time and is misunderstood as the Messiah. As he and the two thieves die in agony on their crosses, he teaches them to sing happy talk. "Always look on the bright side of life."

Why isn't that what Romans 8:28 is saying?

Because it doesn't say everything is good. It says that God makes everything, even evils, work together for our good.

Even that sounds like Dr. Norman Vincent Peale's famous book *The Power of Positive Thinking*. Yet it was written, not by Dr. Peale, but by Dr. Paul, who also believed in evil, Original Sin, divine justice, damnation, Hell,

Satan, and devils. Peale was an idealist; Paul was a re-alist. That's why many people find Peale appealing and Paul appalling. Since I prefer to live in the real world, I find Paul appealing and Peale appalling.

Romans 8:28 cannot possibly mean that everything is good. That's insane. I refute that in three words: Auschwitz, Hiroshima, ISIS.

It's also logically impossible. If everything is good, then it must also be good to deny that everything is good, as most sane people do. If evil is only an illusion, then all our strife and worry about it is unnecessary—and that's even worse!

Of course evil is real. Horribly real. That's what makes this verse so radical. It doesn't say merely that there is good as well as evil or that good is greater than evil or that God makes many good things happen; it says that He makes good come even out of evil. Christians believe He did that two thousand years ago when out of the greatest evil that ever happened, the greatest triumph of Satan, the murder of God incarnate, He brought the greatest good that ever happened, the salvation of mankind. Christians celebrate the deicide on a holiday they call "*Good* Friday". Are Christians incredibly stupid, or is God incredibly clever?

No, not all things are good, but all things "work together for" good. Good is eschatological. At the end of the greatest and most turbulent novel about evil ever written, *The Brothers Karamazov* (the name means "black smear"), the last thing said, after 900+ pages of various hells and purgatories, is "Hurrah for Karamazov."

The existence of evil is by far the strongest argument for atheism. If God is all-good, all-powerful, and all-wise, it seems that evil cannot exist, because if He is all-good, He wills only good, not evil; and if He is all-powerful, He gets whatever He wills; and if He is all-wise, He knows what is truly good and evil. Therefore if God existed, no evil could exist; evil does exist; therefore God does not. Saint Thomas puts the argument most simply: "If one of two contraries [opposites] be infinite, the other would be altogether destroyed. But the word 'God' means that He is infinite goodness. If, therefore, God existed, there would be no evil discoverable; but there is evil in the world. Therefore God does not exist" (*Summa theologica*, I, 2, 3, obj. 1).

And the answer both Augustine and Aquinas (the two greatest Christian minds of all time) give is the same: that God's goodness and power and wisdom are so great that He allows evils to exist in order to bring out of them an even greater good in the end.

This applies to all evils, both the spiritual evil of sins, which come from our free choices, and the physical and emotional evils that come from nature or indirectly from our sins.

In other words, God wrote a novel, not an equation. We are in a great story. That's why the Bible is essentially a narrative interrupted by sermons, not a sermon illustrated by narratives. It's the truth about us, about human life, and that truth is not a timeless truth, like a formula, but a *timely* truth, a true *story*; it "*comes* true". We are not yet at the end of the story.

There's a second reason Romans 8:28 is not Pollyannaism. It doesn't say that all things work together for good *for everybody*, automatically, but only for those who choose to love God, only for those whose "fundamental option" is a "yes" to God, only for those whose deepest will is in line with God's will, only for those who choose "islam" or "surrender" or "abandonment" to God. When you open your heart and soul and life to God, you enter another life, another bloodstream, another cosmic river. This river takes all who swim in it to the sea of Heaven. But not everyone jumps into that river. It's a free choice.

But for those who do make this "leap of faith", all things work together for good, because once we leap into God's will, we leap into pure goodness.

4

An Irrefutable Logical
Proof of Its Truth

If God wills nothing but our best good, and if He has the power always to get what He wills, and if He makes no mistakes about what is in fact our best good, then it necessarily follows, it infallibly follows, it follows with certainty, that all things work together for good for us.

All things, even death. *Especially* death, which is the sum total of all losses, all physical evils. Because death becomes the door to Heaven. The darkest thing in the world becomes the door to the light that is brighter than any light in the world, the light of Heaven, the light that is so bright that God has to give us new eyes to see it because if we saw it with our present eyes, of body and of soul, we would go blind, in body and in soul.

Death is the sum of all physical evils, but it is not the sum of all evils. Spiritual evils are far worse. There are things worse than death. Sin—No to God, alienation from God, divorce from God, refusal of God, who is the source of all good—is far worse than death.

But even sins can be made to work together for good through the golden gate of repentance. For sincerely repented sins can make us humble and wise. That is why God does not give us instant grace to overcome all sins:

because that would make us proud, and pride is the worst sin of all. The Pharisees of Jesus' time seemed more pure and sinless, more obedient to the divine Law, than anyone else; and yet Jesus said they were on the road to Hell because of their one remaining sin, which was more deadly than all other sins put together: the refusal to repent because of pride and self-righteousness. So if you want to attack your other sins, start with attacking your pride.

Saint Augustine, asked to name the four cardinal virtues, replied: Humility, humility, humility, and humility.

~

Romans 8:28 is both the hardest verse in the Bible for us to *believe* to be true and at the same time the most certain verse in the Bible to *be* true. It's the most certain because it necessarily follows from the infinite goodness, power, and wisdom of God, as explained above. Its only alternatives are no God (which is atheism) or a bad, weak, stupid god (which is paganism and idolatry). Yet it is also the hardest to believe because it doesn't *look* like it's true. We don't see all things working together for good. Did Job? Did Jesus' disciples when he was crucified? Of course not. Why not? Because we're not God. That was God's answer to Job. And it was God's sermon to Saint Catherine, in a vision, when He preached the world's shortest sermon in only four words, summarizing all of divine revelation in two two-syllable sentences: "I'm God; you're not." It's amazing how easy it is to forget that last part!

We naturally think that a certain evil ought not to have happened. We are right: evil should not be. But it is. We also naturally think that God ought not to have let it happen. If we had been God, we would not have let it happen. But (stop the presses!) we are not God. We are not only sinful and weak, we are stupid. As God said to Job, He did not notice us standing there when He was designing and creating the universe.

Evil exists. God did not put up a sign in the Garden of Eden reading: "No snake in the grass is permitted here." He did not take away free will from Adam and Eve even when He foresaw that they would eat the forbidden fruit and bring about all the horrible torrent of evils that resulted down through the ages of human history. If we were running the universe, we would surely have done things differently. So there are only two possibilities: either we are wiser than God, or God is wiser than us. Now —assuming that you are not a member of the Supreme Court—tell me which of these two possibilities is the more likely.

Can you believe you are wiser than God? Can you even *want* to believe you are wiser than God, that God is even more stupid than you are? That the world is in the omnipotent hands of a well-intentioned bumbler? A sweet giant with a midget brain? Kierkegaard has a sermon entitled: "On the edification which lies in the thought that we are *always* in the *wrong* before God." If we were ever in the right and God in the wrong, that would be worse than the sun turning to a Black Hole of darkness.

In T. S. Eliot's play *The Cocktail Party*, Celia, a confused modern girl, says to her psychiatrist, who asks her why she came to him, that she hopes that he can convince her that she is insane, "Because if I'm not insane, then the whole world is, and I couldn't live with that." Substitute "God" for "the whole world", and you see the point.

OK, so God is totally trustable because He's always in the right, always in charge, and always in love with us. That justifies Romans 8:28; and Romans 8:28, in turn, justifies the total "abandonment to divine providence" that is the lesson of de Caussade's classic. This "abandonment", or "islam" or "surrender", to God's providential will is also the very essence of holiness.

This holiness is good in three senses of "good". (1) There is a good *reason* for being holy; and (2) it is good to *be* holy, and (3) there are good *consequences* of being holy.

1. There are both good objective reasons for being holy and also good subjective motives for being holy; and these good subjective motives for being holy are based on these good objective reasons for being holy. The reasons are *true*.

2. And being holy, being a saint, is the highest meaning of being good.

3. And the consequences of being holy are *beautiful*. So we have the true, the good, and the beautiful. The three things everyone wants and needs above all other things because they are three attributes of God.

The beautiful consequences of being good are (3a) pleasure, true pleasure, deep pleasure, spiritual pleasure, and, (3b) deeper than pleasure, happiness (which is truer and deeper and more inward and more lasting than pleasure), and, (3c) even deeper than happiness, joy, which is to happiness what happiness is to pleasure.

Evil is real, of course. In fact, life is war, spiritual warfare. But God has won, and won so completely that He makes even evil work for good if we only let Him and trust Him. The whole Christian tradition is full of this teaching about the good that comes from evil, about how God uses evil and suffering to bring about an even greater good and joy for us in the end, as He did on Calvary. The old hymn puts it elegantly: "The flame shall not hurt thee; I only design / Thy dross to consume and thy gold to refine."

That's what God does with our "deepest distress": He "sanctifies" it to us, He sanctifies us by means of it. To "sanctify" is to "make holy".

God makes us holy in two opposite ways, in the two parts of our lives. First, He makes us holy through our own will, our own free choice of faith and hope and love. (For divine grace does not turn off human free will; it turns it on.) And second, He also sanctifies us against our will, through suffering, because the other way of sanctifying us, through our own will's choices, is not strong enough, because our faith and hope and love are not strong enough. So He sanctifies us also through what He allows to happen to us *against* our will, in other words, suffering.

5

How This Truth Changes Your Life

What happens to you when you believe Romans 8:28 and practice the "abandonment" to God that is based on it?

What happens is that you have two things that seem opposite, joy and peace, two of the marks and fruits of the Spirit of God.

On the one hand, you have the excitement of the joy that the world cannot give, the joy of surprise that comes from the unknown, from grace, from gift. This is much greater than mere happiness, which is only the satisfaction of your already-known desires and, therefore, which always eventually gets boring. Joy never does.

You also have the calmness of the "peace that the world cannot give". You have arrived. You are Home, even when you are far away from Home in the valley of the shadow of death, in the turbulent waters of this world's wild rivers. As you walk through this "valley of the shadow of death", this world full of evils both within and without, you "fear no evil", even the evils that are within you, your own weaknesses and follies and fears. You have fears, but you don't fear them! It's even better than F.D.R.'s saying "there is nothing to fear but fear itself", because if F.D.R. is right, there is still one thing to fear, but if Psalm 23 is right, there is nothing to fear.

Why? Because you know that the Lord is "with you" with His rod and His staff, holding your hand as you walk through this dark valley. In fact, He is *carrying* you through it like a lost sheep, cradling you in His own all-powerful hands, which are the hands known to some extent by all religions and which Christians know are also bloody, nail-pierced hands. Like a puppy, you abandon yourself to Him in trustful faith in His fidelity and in tail-wagging hope in His promises and in adoring love of His total lovableness. You do this puppy-thing even in the middle of doing your adult-dog-things, the most active and demanding things that His will and your duties demand you do, like surgery or running a business or fighting a war or making peace between people who distrust and hate and fear each other.

Here's how it works: the trusting look at God overcomes the main obstacle to holiness, which is selfishness. Most selfishness comes from fear of losing or missing something good for yourself, something happifying. Only faith (trust) casts out fear.

Here's the same point, put a little differently. The main obstacle to that joyful, trusting self-surrender is self-love. There is also a good self-love, when you love yourself as God loves you and because God loves you; but the kind of self-love we know best is the bad kind, which C. S. Lewis calls a "rabbit", that is, cowardly, sensual, and worried. The bad self-love is simply "my will be done" instead of "Thy will be done." How can we overcome that rabbit, that habitual egotism, that gap between our will and God's? By believing Romans 8:28; by believing that "trust and obey" will infallibly bring us to joy because

God is omnibenevolent (He wills our greatest joy) and omnipotent (He is able to "work" all things together for that end, since all things are His things, His creation), and omniscient (He never makes mistakes about what really leads to our greatest joy).

In other words, God is not only "nearer to me than I am to myself", as Augustine says, and therefore *knows* me far better than I know myself, but also *loves* me more than I love myself.

Our deepest desire is for both peace and joy. God's deepest desire is also for our peace and joy! We can't lose, because God can't lose! Insofar as we believe that equation, that identity, between His will and ours, we will love His will as we love our own. And insofar as we do that, we will will it. And insofar as we do that, we will become holy.

Of course this is not easy, though it is simple. Nor is it short. It takes time. This is not "fast food religion". Our learning curve is gradual, like a tide. What counts is not so much how far the tide has already come in ("How holy am I?" is not a profitable question), but whether it's an incoming tide or an outgoing tide. Once we put ourselves into God's incoming tide, it is unstoppable. For God is unstoppable. This tide is not driven by our choices and our will, but by His will. We just ride it, like surfers; we just let it carry us. (That is both receptive and active; see chapter 27.) What drives this tide is His will, and His will is not satisfied until this tide of holiness fills every one of our dry little tide pools and caverns and crevices. It will also flatten all our sand castles.

6

God as Your Guru

No one ever became holy on his own. You need a teacher, a spiritual director, a spiritual master, a spiritual father, a guide, a guru. Unfortunately, not everyone can find a helpful human one (I hope you can), but everyone can find a more than helpful divine one. God is your guru.

Hinduism and Buddhism, on the basis of thousands of years of experience, have developed many varied and detailed yoga methods that are psychologically powerful. Your guru chooses for you exactly the yoga that your personality needs and guides you through the use of its often strange and difficult methods. I am not suggesting that we need yoga methods; in fact, all the saints say that the two things that are much less important than we think they are for becoming holy are methods and feelings. But my point is that your relationship with your guru in these religions is instructively similar to your relationship with God in Western religions. It is one of total trust on your part and total authority on his part. The guru often issues bizarre-seeming commands and can be terribly picky about apparently non-spiritual things like posture, breathing, body-part-awareness, eating, drinking, and the arts; but good gurus (there are many fakes) have an uncanny understanding of where you are and what you need psychologically. When you become the guru's student, you become like him: wiser, better, deeper, calmer, more at peace.

The greatest guru is God. Human gurus can take only a few students; God takes on seven billion and gives each one as much personal attention as if he were the only one, 24/7.

How does God "guru" us? By divine providence. By every event in our lives. Jesus assured us that not a single hair falls from our head, and not a single sparrow falls from the sky, without the will of the Heavenly Father. It's Romans 8:28 again. Every single thing that happens in your life is directly and deliberately designed by God for one end: your own personal, individual, unique good, to perfect your unique self, to bring you to maximum joy.

That's why He created the universe! For immortal persons, not for mortal gases and galaxies. Persons alone are of intrinsic value, ends in themselves and not means. Persons alone are willed by God for their own sake. (That was one of Saint John Paul II's favorite quotations from the documents of Vatican II.) Persons alone, of all things in the material universe, are immortal. When galaxies die, all of us will still be young. The universe is an enormously large and complex saint-making machine. Everything else in it, except for us persons, is merely its gears and wheels. And God controls those gears and wheels and steers them all toward the single end of the whole complex machine, and that end is what this book is about: how to be holy. This book is about the purpose not only of your life and all human life but also of the entire 13.7 billion-year-long universe.

In that universe, divine providence is our IEP, our Individualized Education Plan. Nothing is accidental, Nothing is random. Nothing happens by chance. And nothing is "one size fits all", but everything is designed for the individual. Our guru makes no mistakes. He is infallible! Even when His will permits evil things to happen to us, He does so because this is part of what we need. God makes even death work for our greater good in the end. Death, the dark doom that is the consequence of sin, is made into the door to Heavenly light. If He can do that with death, He can certainly do it with any and all of the smaller deaths that are sufferings and losses. They all work for the same end.

This is true not only of the evils we suffer but even for the evils we commit, though in a different way. Even sins serve, if freely and sincerely repented. He deliberately permits them. Of course He could give us the grace to avoid them, but He deliberately withholds it. Why? For the same reason He does everything, for the same reason He banged out the Big Bang, for the same reason He became incarnate and shed His blood: for us, for our greater joy in the end. Or (here is the other theological explanation, which does not contradict the first one), He always does give us sufficient grace (2 Cor 12:9; 1 Cor 10:13), but we refuse it. Could He give us the grace to choose the opposite of refusal? Of course. His arm is not shortened. But He often does not. Why? For the same reason He does everything: because His infinite wisdom sees what we really need, and His infinite love is infinitely single-minded in steering everything toward the end of our maximum joy.

Sometimes we can see His strategy. And when we don't, we can still believe it. He often refuses to help us overcome some obvious sin, like lust or alcoholism or temper, because He knows that pride and self-righteousness and self-satisfaction would be a greater danger for us if He did. Saint Thomas Aquinas compares Him to a doctor who tolerates lesser diseases in order to cure the worse ones. If it were possible for Him to give us better gifts, He would do it. He is not Scrooge. He is infinitely generous. And He never settles for anything less than the best.

Of course it doesn't look that way. All sorts of bad things happen that seem to do no earthly good at all for us. That is exactly what we should expect if He is infinitely wiser than we are. Even a human guru surprises his students. As we surprise our pets. We don't expect our pets to understand the things we do that they find so strange, like taking them to the vet; so why should we expect that we should be able to understand why God does the things He does to us? The gap between our minds and God's is far greater than the gap between our minds and the mind of a dog or a cat. How much can they understand of our mind? Why do you expect we can understand more of God's mind than that?

But even though we cannot *understand* why our guru gives us the unique tasks He does, we can *know* why: because (1) He loves us so much that He wants the very best for us, and (2) He is all-wise in knowing what is really best for us, in the long run, and (3) He is all-powerful in being able to arrange everything just right and to overcome every obstacle to that end.

We will see that in Heaven, when He will let us read more of His mind and see our lives from His perspective, not just ours. We will see the Artist sculpting His masterpiece (us!) stroke by stroke, even as the statue cries out in pain and protest at the chisel.

Though we cannot see that now, we can believe that now. In fact, we *must* believe that now, for the only alternative to this "too good to be true" truth of Romans 8:28 and the only alternative to our abandonment to His providence that puts us into Romans 8:28 and makes it come true for us—the only alternative is either a weak god or a stupid god or a bad god, in other words, no God, for those idols all lack the capital G.

So when you get slapped around by life, you can truly say to God, "Thanks, I needed that." Literally. C. S. Lewis puts it very logically in *A Grief Observed*, reflecting on the agonizing death of his wife from cancer and his own agonizing bereavement: "But is it credible that such extremities of torture should be necessary for us? Well, take your choice. The tortures occur. If they are unnecessary, then there is no God or a bad one. For no even moderately good Being could possibly inflict or permit them if they weren't."

When Jesus prayed, in Gethsemane, "My Father, *if it be possible*, let this chalice [of suffering] pass from me; nevertheless, not as I will, but as you will" (Mt 26:39), he implied that some things are not possible even for an omnipotent God to do. It was not possible, once we had sinned, for God to save both us and Jesus. "Without the shedding of blood there is no forgiveness of sins" (Heb 9:22). Justice is eternal and necessary. Sin has consequences. The only open options are (1) the justice that gives us sin's just consequences and gives Him freedom from them or (2) the stranger justice that is also mercy, which gives freedom for us and lays the consequences of our sins on Him. He performs this great exchange (option 2), but He cannot perform a great ignoring, as if the difference between good and evil, sin and sanctity, Yes and No, did not matter.

So it if were *possible* for God to make us holy and wise by giving us an easier lesson, better gifts, more graces, He certainly would do just that. So if He does not give us the easy way that we would prefer, then it is impossible. (Review C. S. Lewis's logic again, two paragraphs above.) It is not impossible because God's power meets some obstacle, but because it is not intrinsically possible, it is not a meaningful thing at all, *there is nothing there* for God to do. God can actualize any possibility, but some things are not possibilities. "With God all things are possible", but some apparent things are not things at all. For instance, it is not possible for God to force us freely to choose good over evil. Forced freedom is a meaningless self-contradiction, and a meaningless self-contradiction does not magically become meaningful just because you say the words "God can" before it. And what is true of "forced freedom"—that it is literally meaningless because it is self-contradictory and therefore intrinsically impossible —may well be true of many things we wish God would do to us, such as making us saints without suffering.

Our guru is omnipotent, but He is also omniscient and therefore knows what is and is not intrinsically possible. We do not. We often live in unreal worlds, fantasy worlds (like becoming wise and holy without suffering). He never does. That is why we can abandon ourselves completely to Him and to Him alone. We can totally trust this guru.

7

How Divine Providence
Does What Seems Impossible

But how can God guru all of us at once? How can He write a good plot for a story with over seven billion protagonists, each of which interacts in countless indirect ways with every other one? What is good for one person is bad for another. How can He make even evil things work for good *for all*, or at least for all of those who love Him and abandon themselves to His providence?

It's hard enough to understand how He can do this with physical evils but even harder with moral evils. For moral evils like murder, theft, rape, and adultery are not good for anybody. They are bad both for the perpetrator and for the victim. True, we sometimes repent and learn from our sins, as we often learn from our sufferings, but not always. How can God write a perfect story with such imperfect characters? The poet says that "God writes straight with crooked lines." But how is that possible?

No one but God can answer that question.

But we can answer another question: the question of why we can't answer the first question, the question of how God can do this. And the answer is given by God Himself to Job. The answer is in the form of a question: Why did you suppose you *could* answer that question? You're not God. (Incredibly, we keep forgetting that!) We're not the Author of the story; we're a few of the many characters in it. Why should Rosencrantz and Guildenstern know what Shakespeare is up to in *Hamlet*?

So the answer to the question of why we should believe Him when God tells us that "for those who love God all things work together for good" is: Because He's God, and we're not. He's God, and He does not make mistakes, and He inspired Saint Paul to tell us this precious and amazing truth in Romans 8:28. Do you really want to correct Him? Will you be God's teacher instead of His pupil? Will you be His copyeditor instead of His reader? Do you want to edit His mail before you deliver it? Did you write the Bible? Did you design the saint-making machine that is the universe?

But we can see clues in nature to the truths of Scripture. For the same God wrote both books, nature and Scripture. God's mind invented the physical universe, and we are constantly discovering more and more of its intricate and amazing intelligence and perfection. For instance, the multifaceted, multidimensional "anthropic principle": if the four fundamental forces of physics had been aligned the slightest bit differently, atoms could never have formed. If the temperature of the primeval fireball had been a millionth of a degree hotter or colder a millionth of a second after the Big Bang, carbon could never have come to form and no life could ever have existed anywhere in the universe. If our earth had had no moon, and thus no tides, animal life never could have evolved in the oceans. If water had gotten heavier rather than lighter when it froze, like all other elements, aquatic life would have died and terrestrial life could not have evolved. If the sun had been a little hotter or colder, or if the earth had not rotated, it would have been too cold and/or too hot for life. Etc., etc.—there are dozens of these astronomically enormous "coincidences", alignments, windows of opportunity for human life, each of which had to open just exactly so much, not even the tiniest bit more or less. If the Creator can design such an incredibly super-intelligent and perfect *setting* for His drama of human life and history, is it reasonable to think He cannot also arrange a super-intelligent and perfect *plot*? Is He only a perfect mathematician and physicist but not a perfect psychologist and novelist? Is His super-intelligence limited to a statically perfect map of the physical setting instead of extending also to the characters and the plot? Even a plot of a wild, dramatic, messy, and astonishingly complex set of interactions among free human beings?

8

Faith and Reason: Can We Believe It if We Don't Understand It?

Faith and reason do not contradict each other, but they cannot substitute for each other, either. They are like men and women that way. So reason cannot substitute for faith. There has to be room for faith alone, and for both, and for reason alone. There has to be room for faith alone regarding the mysteries of God's mind and providence, because if we understood it all, there would be no room to believe it. That's why God deliberately hides both from our senses and our reason: to make room for our faith. Hearts are more precious than eyes or even brains. Brains cannot substitute for hearts. Lovers do not propose in syllogisms. They say to each other: "Trust me. Abandon yourself to me. Surrender. Throw yourself into my arms." They say to each other what God says to us.

Understanding *how* God can providentially provide the best for each of His children when they are all immersed in this mysterious, messy global plot—understanding how Romans 8:28 can be possible—is not necessary for us. De Caussade says: "Holiness is produced in us by the will of God and our acceptance of it. It is not produced by intellectual speculation about it. If we are thirsty we must have a drink and not worry about books which explain what thirst is" (p. 25). Do we need to know the chemistry of water before we can slake our thirst? But we cannot slake our thirst until we drink, and we cannot drink until we trust. Faith, in every other area of life, comes first, before understanding. How insane to think that it should not come first when it comes to understanding the ways of the infinitely wise God!

In Tolstoy's autobiography, *Confession*, he tells this parable:

> If I will not do what is asked of me, then I will never understand what is asked of me. . . .
>
> If a naked, hungry beggar should be taken from the crossroads and led into an enclosed area in a magnificent establishment to be given food and drink, and if he would then be made to move some kind of lever up and down, it is obvious that before determining why he was brought there to move the lever and whether the structure of the establishment was reasonable, the beggar must first work the lever. If he will work it, then he will see that it operates a pump, that the pump draws up water, and that the water flows into a garden. Then he will be taken from the enclosed area and set to another task, and then he will gather fruits and enter into the joy of his lord. . . .
>
> Thus the simple, uneducated working people, whom we look upon as animals, do the will of their master without ever reproaching him. But we, the wise, consume everything the master provides without doing what he asks of us; instead, we sit in a circle and speculate on why we should do something so stupid as moving this lever

up and down. And we have hit upon an answer. We have figured it out that either the master is stupid or he does not exist, while we alone are wise.[1]

C. S. Lewis writes: "There are only two kinds of people in the end: those who say to God, 'Thy will be done,' and those to whom God says, in the end, '*Thy* will be done'" (*The Great Divorce*). The difference is made by our choice. In order to find death rather than life in the end, in order to go to Hell, you must be insane: you must choose misery over joy. Why would you do that? Because you can understand and control misery but not joy. This is insane. But it is what we all do in some degree whenever we sin. For all sin is choosing misery over joy. We are all insane. That is what Original Sin means.

But God deeply loves His severely brain-damaged children. If He did not, we would have no hope. But He does, and therefore we do.

Sanctity is only sanity, that is, living in the real world. The real world is the world where God is present everywhere as He really is, that is, as God, the omnibenevolent, omniscient, and omnipotent center, beginning, and end of everything; as the omnibenevolent, all-loving, all-giving Creator and Designer of everything in our story; as the omniscient, providential plot-director of everything that happens in it; and as the omnipotent power that moves everything on stage toward a perfect end.

That is either true or not. If that is not true, then let us

[1] Leo Tolstoy, *Confession*, trans. David Patterson (New York: W. W. Norton, 1983), 70–71.

all become atheists, so that we can live in the real world and not in illusion and fantasy. If it is true, then let us become saints for exactly the same reason.

So at least let us be reasonable. God says: "Come now, let us reason together" (Is 1:18). Nothing is more reasonable than living in reality. And the only way to do that is to be holy.

9

Why Surrender Does Not
Squash Individuality

But would not such providential "plotting" of the whole story of human life on earth necessarily mean ignoring individuality? For even if we grant that God is writing a single perfect novel, must not the perfection of the whole be achieved at the expense of the perfection of its parts? What is good for one person is not necessarily good for another; so when writing the drama of human life, must not God use some of His characters for the sake of others, as a human dramatist uses "walk-ons", not for their own sake, but to better define and set off the important characters? And must not our total submission to that divine providence therefore surrender our unique individuality? Don't you have to be something of a rebel to assert your individuality? Does God want limp doormats as His saints?

No. Even we can do better than that, as every parent who has at least two children knows. You don't have to sacrifice what is best for one of your children for what is best for another one. Even when you can't split things equally, like parts of a pie, and when the older kids get the new clothes while the younger kids get the hand-me-downs, the younger kids get the advantage of having big brothers and sisters. There is not equality (how dull!), but there is reciprocity.

As with the sexes. Men and women are not equal in nature, only in ultimate value. Men are vastly superior to women—at being men. And women are vastly superior to men—at being women. Denial of that blatantly obvious fact is part of the insanity of the "sexual revolution". If you dare to face this "the sky is blue" truth today, you lose your job. (Ask the ex-president of Harvard, Larry Summers.) The only real sexual equality is the equality of two inequalities. And out of this relationship, which God invented, this relationship that is infinitely more complex, unpredictable, dramatic, interesting, and joyful than the relationship of equality, comes most of our great poems, songs, operas, dances, paintings, epics, and novels. In this relationship, surrender *fulfills* individuality. It happens! At what moment do two lovers find themselves most completely? At the moment they lose themselves most completely in each other.

Far from ignoring, downplaying, or threatening our unique individuality, God's providence deliberately designs for it. For, as de Caussade says, "God . . . manifests his will so differently to each of us" (p. 78). And C. S. Lewis says:

> If He had no use for all these differences, I do not see why He should have created more souls than one. Be sure that the ins and outs of your individuality are no mystery to Him; and one day they will no longer be a mystery to you. . . . [In Revelation 2:17, God says:] "To him that overcometh I will give a white stone, and in the stone a new name written, which no man knoweth

saving he that receiveth it." What can be more a man's own than this new name which even in eternity remains a secret between God and him? And what shall we take this secrecy to mean? Surely, that each of the redeemed shall forever know and praise some one aspect of the Divine beauty better than any other creature can. Why else were individuals created? . . . For doubtless the continually successful, yet never complete, attempt by each soul to communicate its unique vision to all others (and that by means whereof earthly art and philosophy are but clumsy imitations) is also among the ends for which the individual was created.[1]

God integrates all these irreducible differences between individuals into a single plot that perfects every one of them. Every one of them, at least, who consents to it, who accepts God, whose heart utters a fundamental Yes rather than No to Him, who chooses faith and hope and love rather than mistrust, despair, and misery.

But how is this possible?

We do not know God's mind from above or from within it, but we have clues and analogies from below, from nature. One is the relation between light and color. The same light perfects and reveals the unique individuality of every color, so that the more light shines on blue or green or red, the bluer the blue and the greener the green and the redder the red. (Remember how fascinating the unique individuality of each color was to you when you were very young?) If you had been born blind, you would not have been able to imagine this amazing

[1] C. S. Lewis, *The Problem of Pain* (San Francisco: HarperCollins, 2001), 151, 154–55.

achievement of light. And compared to God's mind, we are all blind.

And God's mind does this not only to colors but to all things created. Since God's mind transcends finite things, it perfects all finite things. What it does to comets and cats and colors it does to human persons. It does it to you, whenever you choose to stand in this light.

We have another remote analogy in salt. Suppose you had never tasted salt. Suppose now that someone tried to describe its effects to you: "Salt makes steak taste steakier and fish taste fishier and eggs taste eggier." "The same salt?" "Yes." "Impossible." "No. Try it, you'll like it."

The salt analogy is weaker than the light analogy because it's possible to drown out any other taste by too much salt. For salt has its own peculiar taste, as light does not have its own peculiar color. But though it is a weak analogy, it is a real one. It is true to a very small extent.

A still better one is thought. Thought is infinite with relation to things: we can think any thinkable thing at all. But thought does not pervert or harm or ignore things when it knows them; it gives them a second life, in the mind of the thinker. What our thought does to physical things God's thought does to our personalities.

De Caussade proves from biblical history that obedience to the Will of God perfects rather than thwarts individuality, by specific cases. He says that this obedience "produced Abel, Noah and Abraham—all different types. Isaac is also original. Jacob is not a duplicate of him, nor is Joseph a facsimile of Jacob. Moses is different from his ancestors. David and the prophets bear no resemblance to the patriarchs. John the Baptist stands alone" (p. 82).

The supreme model for this total surrender is Jesus Himself, of course. His perfect surrender did not make Him a dullard, a dishrag, or a doormat. It made Him a fire, like the fire from the Burning Bush. He *is* the fire from the Burning Bush, the fire that did not destroy but enlightened and surprised and revealed and changed everyone who met Him. So unique is His personality that no one has ever succeeded in writing a credible fictional story about Him. Yet He was the greatest "conformist" to God's Will who ever lived. He said that He had come into the world "not to do my own will, but the will of him who sent me" (Jn 6:38). He never claimed to be "original" and, therefore, was the most original man who ever lived. This perfect Muslim, this perfect submitter, or surrenderer, this total "conformist", was the most free, unique, individualized, fully realized human personality that has ever existed—not despite His conformity, but precisely because of it.

When Jesus said, in Gethsemane, "Not my will, but yours, be done", that would have been cheap if He had had little or no will of His own to surrender. The words would have been meaningless and the gift would have been impossible if He had not had a will of His own to surrender, a human personality to submit. The greater the surrender, the greater the individual personality can be. And the greater the individual personality, the greater the surrender can be.

10

Where to Find God:
The Practice of the Presence of God

"Surely the LORD is in this place; and I did not know it", said Jacob after his vision of the ladder from Heaven to earth with angels ascending and descending on it like commercial traffic on a superhighway at commuter time (Gen 28:16).

But this is true of every place. And "the practice of the presence of God", in Brother Lawrence's felicitous and unforgettable phrase, the habit of seeing God everywhere (by faith, of course, not by sight), is a most effective angel on that ladder, a most powerful vehicle on the road to being a saint, because it is a foretaste, however dim, of the Beatific Vision in Heaven, when we shall see God face to face. Who could ever sin while gazing on Infinite Beauty and Goodness, when all the Devil's fogs and lies are gone and you see, with absolute clarity, that Goodness is beautiful and irresistibly attractive and Evil is ugly and impotent even to tempt you? No one. That is why there will be no sin in Heaven even though we will not lose our free will.

In other words, Plato's famous teaching that all evil is only ignorance is true except for time and place. It will be true after death in Heaven, but it is not true yet, on earth.

Plato famously claimed that all vice was ignorance and all virtue was knowledge, so that the highest know-ledge, philosophical wisdom, was the inevitable cause of moral goodness. His reasonable-seeming reason for this unreasonable-seeming conclusion was as follows: if only we clearly knew, all the time and without doubt, that only virtue made us happy and vice always made us miserable, then we would always choose virtue and never vice, because we always choose happiness and never misery. Our constant choice of happiness would become a constant choice of virtue if we had the wisdom to see their identity. For we always choose the apparent good —if a thing does not appear good in some way to us, it is psychologically impossible to choose it or even to like it. So all we need to become saints is the wisdom to distinguish the apparent good from the real good. True philosophy will make you a saint.

Plato's teaching sounds very logical in the abstract, but we all know from experience that it doesn't work that way. We often know quite clearly that X is evil and Y is good; that X is not only evil in the sense of disobedience to God but also evil in the sense of harmful to ourselves and a cause of our misery. Yet we do evil. We choose what we know will lead to misery over what we know will lead to joy. Why? Because we are not rational; we are ad-dicted. We are sinaholics. Any addiction makes you crazy, including the master addiction to getting your own way.

Yet there is a profound half-truth in Plato. What he says is true of Heaven, but not of earth. It is not true of earth because it is impossible to have that clear Heavenly sight on earth; the Devil's deceptions are powerful, and he camouflages his ugly fishhook with very attractive worms to get us to bite it. For another thing, our passions are disordered and are stronger than our reason. For still another thing, our will is weak, so even when we see the truth, we often do not will it. So there are three reasons Plato is wrong: because our reason, our passions, and our will are all fallen.

But *insofar as* we can see the truth and the true beauty of goodness, we find it much easier to be holy. And the most effective "insofar as" is not an abstract philosophical argument, like Plato's, no matter how logical it is, but the concrete experience of an example of it, like the joy in the face of a saint, the beauty of an act of selfless love, like Christ's, or the experienced presence of the God whose Goodness and Beauty are as inseparable as the Divine Person is inseparable from the Divine Nature. That's what we will see in Heaven, and that's what we can aspire to "see" at least with the eyes of faith here on earth. That's what Jacob saw when he said "How holy is this place!"

When and where can we see God? God is everywhere (He is ubiquitous, or omnipresent, not limited to place) and everywhen (He is eternal, not limited to time); and therefore, in order to live in reality, we must see and find Him everywhere and everywhen, in what de Caussade calls "the sacrament of the present moment"; that is, we must "practice the presence of God" everywhere and everywhen, as Brother Lawrence says. The essential spiritual task given to us by both of these very simple and holy men is the same.

That "seeing" God everywhere and everywhen, that "sacrament of the present moment", that "practicing the presence of God", is the single most effective aid to becoming holy that I know, from all three sources of knowledge: my own experience, my faith, and my reason.

Another word for it is "prayer". It is our umbilical cord to God. It can and should become habitual. There are many ways to obey Saint Paul's advice to "pray constantly" (1 Thess 5:17).

It is also our foretaste of Heaven. In Heaven we will "practice the presence of God" eternally. We will be like Jacob and see everything—literally everything—as a ladder, a road, a relationship between ourselves and God. Since that is what we are designed and destined to do forever, we had better get some practice in now.

Life on earth is rehearsal. The meaning of life on earth is life in Heaven, exactly as the meaning of life in the womb is life on earth. When we die and pop out of this universe as we popped out of the womb when we were born, we will look back on this world, on this whole universe, as a little womb. And we will see that just as the fetus was in the world as soon as it was conceived, long before it was born, because the womb was the beginning of the world, even though the fetus could not see that, so we were in Heaven as soon as we were baptized and "born again", even though we could not see it while we were in Heaven's womb, this little universe.

This vision of God's presence is the vision of the Song of Songs. In that mystical poem the human bride sings of her divine lover: "Behold, here he stands behind our wall, gazing in at the windows, looking through the lattice" (Song 2:9). The "wall" is the wall of the senses, which we can pierce a little by reason and a little more by faith. The "windows" are the windows of His omniscience, which turns all our opaque walls into transparent windows for His all-seeing eyes. The "lattice" is the lattice of our half-light, half-dark lives, our fog, our "in a mirror dimly" (1 Cor 13:12). He is mystery to us; but we are no mystery to Him.

Our ignorance is our protection. We naturally wonder why He does not reveal Himself more clearly and totally to us. And the answer is: Because "his immediate presence would terrify us", as de Caussade says (p. 94). We would dissolve, like fog in sunlight. It would kill us, as the fire of a volcano kills a gnat. If you don't know that, you don't know God. "Our God is a consuming fire" (Heb 12:29). That's why we have to learn to become more solid, more real: so that we can endure that light, that fire. That's why God gave us moral law on earth: for what C. S. Lewis calls "the thickening treatment" (*The Great Divorce*).

Catholics call completion of that thickening process "Purgatory". Call it what you will, but if you really think that you can endure and enjoy the full light and fire of God a second after you die, being essentially the same kind of being you are now, without any additional divine operations on your soul, then you dangerously underestimate either your sinful nature or God's holiness or the gap between them.

And that's one of the reasons why He assumes disguises now. "All these things [are] the disguise God assumes", says de Caussade (p. 94). What things? All things, except sin. All material things and events in our lives, and all the spiritual events, too. And all the ugly, bothersome people we meet, first of all in ourselves. He is there, too, and "As you did to one of the least of these my brethren, you did it to me" (Mt 25:40).

11

Overcoming Deism
and the Absentee God

In the previous chapter, we saw that the relation between the supernatural and the natural is like the relationship between light and color. A well-known formula in theology says that "grace (the supernatural) perfects nature." It does not ignore it, bypass it, subvert it, demean it, rival it, or destroy it. One example: the light of supernatural faith sharpens and clarifies the light of natural reason. Another example: the supernatural love of charity (*agapē*) perfects the natural loves, friendship (*philia*), passion (*eros*), and spontaneous liking (*storge*). Another: when the will frees itself from the slavery to the passions and says "your will be done" to God, when the will lets God rule the passions, the passions become happier and healthier and stronger, not weaker. Still another example: faithfully married people have more satisfying sex lives than playboys and playgirls. Still another: priests and monks and nuns who give up the world live the longest in it. Ask any insurance company.

As light is transcendent to all colors, God is transcendent to all finite creatures. And just as light is also immanent to or present to and perfective of all colors, so God is also immanent to and present to and perfective of all creatures. In fact, He can be immanent, or omnipresent, precisely *because* He is transcendent, like light.

Because of this paradox of God's transcendence and immanence, two heresies are possible. We can deny either half of the paradox for the sake of the other. We can easily think that if God is transcendent, He must be far away; and if He is present, He must be just another one of us or maybe all of us at once. Deism denies God's immanence, or presence, and pantheism and paganism deny God's transcendence. Thus pantheism and paganism do not believe God literally created everything else out of nothing. Paganism says that god (or more usually gods in the plural) is one of the things in nature, and pantheism says that he (or she or it) is all of them or the indwelling soul of all of them. Deism, at the other extreme, denies his immanence. Thus its god is long ago and far away, not here and now. He created the world long ago but then left if far behind, and if he rules it, he rules it like an absentee landlord. And like a deadbeat dad he doesn't even visit his kids any more.

Americans tend to be deists, like many of our Founding Fathers, especially Jefferson. The practical problem with deism, the reason deism makes it hard to be holy, is that we can't get close enough to the divine Source of holiness (God Himself) to become holy by having it rub off on us.

But God is not far away. That is not what "transcendence" means. Nor is He near by, being just one of the many finite things or persons in the universe. That is not what "immanence" means. He is neither outside the universe nor inside it; nor is He either outside us or inside us. Both it and we are in Him. Where we are does not define where He is. We are relative to Him, not He to us. Thus, after Adam falls, He asks him, "Where are you now?" (Gen 3:9). The universe does not give Him His address: He gives it its. It is "the creation", *His* creation. It is relative to Him, not He to it. When He gave Lady Julian of Norwich one of her "showings" (visions), she saw a tiny hazelnut held in a giant hand. "What is that nut?" she asked Him. He answered: "It is all that is made." In other words, "He's got the whole world in His hands."

What does this theology have to do with becoming holy? De Caussade tells us: "All is in the hand of God. His action is vaster and more pervasive than all the elements of earth, air and water. It [His action, His providence] enters through every one of your senses. . . . God's action penetrates every atom of your body. . . . The blood flowing through your veins moves only by his will . . . all your bodily conditions are the working of his grace" (p. 53). Saint Augustine says that God is nearer to us than we are to ourselves.

Grace (God's supernatural action) is not an afterthought, an addition to nature. It is there from the beginning. We can find Him in all things because He is in all things. Or, more accurately, all things are in Him. Grace is not in nature so much as nature is in grace. Saint Thérèse said, on her deathbed, "Everything is grace."

What is nature, then? It is the nature of grace.

We imagine God (or His angel) coming closer to us as a thin cloud of light that comes to permeate thicker things because it is so thin. We think of spirit as thinner than matter. No, it is thicker. When God (or His angel) comes closer to us, it is like an iron ball moving through a cloud. He permeates thin things because He is so thick.

If that analogy didn't grab you, forget it.

God is not a part of our life; we are parts of His. He is not the object of our religious experience; we are the objects of His.

The things in the world are parts of a great picture that God is painting, notes in a great piece of music that God is singing, words in a great poem that God is speaking, events in a great story that God is writing. The next time you see a butterfly or a mosquito, remember that it is a word that God is speaking. For, as de Caussade says, "things proceed like words from the mouth of God. For what God creates at each moment is a divine thought [an inner word] which is expressed by a thing, and so all these things are so many names and words" (p. 49). The cataract of gases and galaxies and geese and girls is a cataract of words that stream like a waterfall of millions of meanings from God's infinitely creative mind, words that are turned into matter. That is why nature is holy and why it can make us holy: because God is there, as Beethoven is in every note of every piece of music he composed.

How does nature make us holy? Only if we see it as it is. What does that mean? This is what it means: when the Great King sends His ambassador to your house with a message, sealed with His personal King's seal and addressed to you personally, how do you treat that ambassador and that letter and that moment? The messenger is God's angel ("angel" *means* "messenger"), and the letter is all the things that God made and did and said, and the moment is now.

What things? Events, which come from a long line of human causes extending back through the human family to Adam. And things in nature like sunlight and wind that come to us from Him down an even longer line of causes extending back through the universe to the Big Bang ("Let there be light!"). They are all parts of Jacob's Ladder. Jacob's Ladder is everything—everything except God, at the top, and you, at the bottom. The Ladder includes other people. You are part of their Jacob's Ladder as they are part of yours.

A ladder has two sides and many rungs. Jacob's Ladder's two sides are time and space, and its rungs are material things and events. That is why God invented time: so that we could find Him in it. That is why God invented space: to give us a place to find Him. That is why God invented matter: to make spiritual things visible to us, to make Himself known to material creatures.

So matter is holy, and space is holy, and time is holy. The present moment (which is the only real time) is holy. Everything is holy. Only sinful man is not holy. That is why we must become what everything else is—holy: so that we can take our place, our privileged place, in this roaring river of beauty, God's creation.

So reverence the things that God sends to you in the present moment, which is His letter. And reverence the present moment itself, which is His ambassador.

Here is a simple personal example. I find the sea the most beautiful thing in the material world. Perhaps for you it is the stars or sunsets or symphonies or flowers or babies. When I don't see the sea for months, I dry up and get antsy. Then I sit on a rock for an hour just watching waves and smiling and listening to them; and that makes it a lot easier and more natural for me to listen to God, and *that* makes it easier to listen to other people, an art that I find bothersomely hard to do since I am by temperament impatient and a "loner", with ADD. God put a strange power into nature (the Iroquois call it "orenda") to make our hearts calmer and happier and even holier. Use it.

12

The Epistemology of Holiness

Holiness is as much a matter of seeing as it is a matter of trying; as much a matter of thinking as it is of willing. But the seeing that makes us holy is not seeing with the first eye, the eyes of the body. Nor is it seeing with the second eye, the eye of the reason. It is seeing with the third eye, the eye of the heart. And that seeing is called faith (and also hope, and also love, which are all parts of one attitude, which de Caussade calls "abandonment").

De Caussade says: "Our faith is never more alive than when what we experience through our senses [apparently] contradicts it and tries to destroy it" (p. 37). The same is true of our feelings, which are our internal senses. Seeing and feeling are good and give us much truth and joy; but God deliberately hides from our senses and usually also from our feelings in order to strengthen our faith. He hides from our outer eye in order to exercise our inner eye. De Caussade says: "By our senses we can see only the actions of the creature, but faith sees the creator acting in all things" (p. 34).

Faith does not blind itself to things; it looks along them instead of looking at them; it reads them as signs, as words spoken by God. Once we look along things instead of just looking at them, we "see" God everywhere, with the eyes of faith. For He is really there, but veiled. De Caussade says: "The actions of created beings are veils which hide the profound mysteries of the workings of God" (p. 34). He is there, but He is holding up a thick rug behind which He is hiding. The rug is the material appearance of everything in the universe. Thus "we know the truth without seeing it" with either senses, reason, or feeling.

Faith is not a feeling, faith is a knowing that is deeper than rational knowing. Faith is like a rock; feelings are like waves. They are lots of fun to play in (and sometimes scary and painful when they whomp you), but you cannot live in them, and you cannot build on them anything solid and lasting.

The very lack of emotional excitement in faith can be deeply exciting: faith knows that there's Somebody there, and He's hiding! At death, He will pop out like a jack in the box and inhabit our seeing and our feeling like a conquering king returning to his rightful throne. Until then, "we walk by faith and not by sight."

There is a moral dimension to this. "The duties of each moment are shadows which hide the action of the divine will" (p. 21). Duties—the driest and dullest and dustiest and least "sexy" of all moral categories—are our divine guru's training in preparation for the mystical ecstasy for which we are all designed. Duties are disguises of spiritual foreplay.

This vision radically changes our relations to our neighbors, for most of our duties are to our neighbors. These duties, and our neighbors themselves, are disguises worn by God. De Caussade says: "If we know that someone in disguise is really our king, we shall behave very differently toward him . . . the clothing is shabby and mean to the ordinary eye, but we shall respect the royal majesty hidden under it" (p. 36). As C. S. Lewis says, "Next to the Blessed Sacrament itself, your neighbour is the holiest object presented to your senses. If he is your Christian neighbour, he is holy in almost the same way, for in him Christ *vere latitat* [truly hides]" (*The Weight of Glory*). As Christ himself said, "As you did to one of the least of these my brethren, you did it to me." Especially the least, for He especially disguises Himself "in the distressing disguise of the poor", as Mother Teresa used to say. If we only saw Who was there . . .

How important for holiness is the intelligence, then?

That depends on what kind of intelligence you mean. Factual knowledge is irrelevant; holiness is not a quiz show. General IQ and cleverness are irrelevant; holiness is not dependent on Harvard or Mensa. There have been some brilliant saints (Augustine, Aquinas), some very bright saints (More, Newman), some very ordinary saints (Philip Neri, Francis of Assisi, Francis de Sales), and some saints who seldom used words of more than one syllable (Joseph of Cupertino, Mother Teresa of Calcutta). All of them see with the eye of faith in the heart, with the intelligence of the heart, which, Pascal famously said, "has its reasons, which the reason does not know". It is this seeing with the heart that is a most powerful aid to sanctity.

But what does "heart" mean?

We have to distinguish four different meanings.

1. Sometimes "heart" means intellectual intuition, as in Pascal.

2. Sometimes "heart" means the emotions, the feelings. Many human emotions we share with animals, for instance: anger, fear, spontaneous liking or disliking, comfort, discomfort, pain, pleasure, and the instinct to aid others of our species. Other emotions are specifically human, for instance: *righteous* anger, not just at inconvenience, but at injustice; respectful fear, not just servile fear; deliberate approval or disapproval; the peace that the world cannot give; spiritual agony and ecstasy; and personal compassion. These are as much a part of the image of God in us, a part of our immortal souls, as the intellect and the will are. (See Dietrich von Hildebrand's little classic *The Heart*.)

3. Sometimes "heart" means "will", which is the captain of the soul and which commands the intellect to look or not to look, and (with much less success) tries to command the emotions to turn on (usually with little or no success) or off (with only a little more success). This is where essential love resides: essential love is an act of will, the will to the good of another. That is the only reason God can *command* us to love. Emotions cannot be commanded. It matters absolutely, it matters enormously, whether we love God and neighbor with our will —in fact, it matters eternally. It matters only relatively whether we love with the emotions. Emotions can be a powerful aid to willing. They can also be a powerful obstacle to willing. They are also natural effects of willing: the more you will good to your neighbor, the more compassion you feel toward him; the less you will his good, the easier it is to feel indifference or cruelty. So emotions

are very important, but not so much for themselves as for
their aid to willing.

4. Finally, "heart" often means the mysterious source
and center of everything in the soul, as the physical organ that pumps the blood is the source of life (through
the blood) throughout the body. This is what Scripture
usually means by "heart". It is impossible to define because it is not a wedge of the circle but the dimensionless
point at its center; not an object to be mapped, but the
subject doing the mapping; not one of the distinguish-
able powers of the soul, but the "I" whose powers they
are. For we speak of "my" mind, "my" will, "my" emotions. My "heart" is the "I" who possesses them. On
two occasions the New Testament calls it "spirit" and
distinguishes it from "soul" (1 Thess 5:23; Heb 4:12).
Solomon in his Proverbs says "Keep your heart with all
vigilance; for from it flow the springs of life" (Prov 4:23).
It is the source of our thinking, willing, and feeling; the
pre-functional root of all the functions. This is the deepest meaning of "heart".

When Scripture uses "heart", it sometimes means specifically human emotions like compassion; sometimes it
means "will"; sometimes it means intellectual intuition;
and most often it means that mysterious center of the self
that is our "I", the center in us of the image of the "I
am" that is God. Only you and God have that name. We
are forbidden to make graven images of God not only
because God is not material but also because God has already made the only true images of Himself: us.

The first eyes, the eyes of the body, relate us to the

physical world, the world of matter. The second eyes, the
eyes of the mind, relate us to the mental world, the world
of forms, of essences, of *logoi*, of ideas, of meanings. (Animals cannot enter that world, though they tremble on
its brink.) The third eye, the eye of the heart, relates us
to God.

The practical point about holiness that this map of the
soul helps to explain is that the eye of the heart can to
some extent compensate for our weakness of will, our
divided will. We all love creatures too much and God
too little, ourselves too much and God and our neighbors too little. The eye of the heart can compensate for
this somewhat for a very simple reason: because if we see
God better, it will be easier to love Him. And if we see
Him in our neighbor, whom He created in His image
and in whose soul He wants to live and whom He loves
and commands us to love—if we see Him there, we will
much more easily love Him there.

For He is beautiful, and seeing beauty naturally leads
to loving beauty, wherever we see it. And loving something beautiful with our emotions naturally (but not in-
evitably) leads to loving it with our will and our deepest heart. The obvious example is romantic love. Since
beauty of soul is expressed in the beauty of the acts of the
body, especially the face, we can be led, if we will, from
the physical signs to the spiritual beauty of the person
that these signs signify.

We should apply what we know about the power of
romantic love to the goal of holiness. We should see holiness as "sexy". For human sexuality, too, is part of the
image of God (Gen 2:7 says that!) and is spiritual as well

as physical, unlike merely animal sex. It is inexcusable that when we want to be holy and when we look around for the most effective and powerful analogies and examples from which to learn, we ignore the most powerful passion in the world. But the saints and mystics have not ignored it; it has been their favorite analogy, metaphor, and image ever since the "Song of Songs" was written, about twenty-five hundred years ago.

This analogy is the heart of Saint John Paul II's "Theology of the Body", the Church's answer to the Sexual Revolution. God's Church always redeems and uplifts and beautifies what God has created and designed, especially when sinful mankind perverts, degrades, and uglifies it.

13

Little Things

Saint Thérèse says: "I have no other means of proving my love for you than that of . . . profiting by all the smallest things and doing them through love."[1] James Hudson Taylor says: "A little thing is a little thing, but faithfulness in little things is a great thing."[2] Little things are not big, but doing little things with big love is big. In fact, the very fact that little things are only little is part of the reason why it's so big to do them with big love.

Notice that Saint Thérèse is not denying that little things are little and big things are big. She is not denying objective truth. But she is implying that there is another dimension that is even more important: the subjective truth of obedient love.

The doing is bigger than the thing done. That's why doing big things with little love is only little, but doing little things with big love is big. Doing is not a thing.

Men tend to think more about things, women about doing. That's why men more often treat women as things

---

[1] *Story of a Soul: The Autobiography of St. Thérèse of Lisieux*, trans. John Clarke, O.C.D. (Washington, D.C.: ICS Publications, Institute of Carmelite Studies, 1976), 196.

[2] A. J. Broomhall, *Hudson Taylor and China's Open Century*, Book 4 (London: Hodder and Staughton and Overseas Missionary Fellowship, 1984, 154).

than women treat men as things. Men tend to like fighting and conquering the world of things. Women specialize in persons and relationships. That's why women tend to personify things and to "take things personally" more than men do. Women and men have different but equal plusses and minuses. Everyone always knew that, until we made ourselves stupid with modern sex education.

Women understand Saint Thérèse's point about sanctity better than men do. Women don't get to fight wars, win heavyweight championships, or become fictional superheroes as much as men do. Throughout history, their lives have centered around children and home: cooking, cleaning, changing diapers, kissing boo boos. That is a fact, whether you interpret it as natural and right or as unnatural and wrong. So this aspect of holiness is one where men need to learn from women.

Men can also learn this same lesson from sports, which has traditionally been more of a man's concern than a woman's. In every sport, defense wins games, even though offense is more spectacular, obvious, interesting, and spectator-riveting. In baseball, "good pitching (the essence of defense) beats good hitting (the essence of offense)." Any football, soccer, or basketball coach will tell you the same thing: that defense, the unspectacular aspect of the game, determines who wins most of the time.

The same is true in life (since sports imitate life). Spectacular heroism, even martyrdom, is easy; the daily grind is hard. Many can respond to emergencies heroically; few can keep up their charity day to day, especially when no one notices. That's why picking up a scrap of paper for the love of God can be more of a proof of sanctity than martyrdom.

When that is done, the extraordinary and supernatural (God living with man) does not sink to the ordinary and merely natural level, but the ordinary and natural is raised to the extraordinary and supernatural. As de Caussade says, "thus, the commonplace becomes extraordinary" (p. 115). It is the most extraordinary "splendor in the ordinary". The Athanasian Creed says that the Incarnation happened, not by the conversion of divinity into humanity, but by the raising of humanity into divinity.

Every kind of energy takes the form of waves. On the sea, a wave's power is not on its crest, where it is most visible and most spectacular, but in its trough. The same is true of emotions. God's Spirit is most powerfully at work in us during emotional troughs, the "dry" times, not the "high" times. All the saints teach that. When the aid of feelings is removed, we can move forward only by heroic effort of our will. This is an especially crucial lesson today because it is so countercultural. The Romantics have corrupted us into thinking that feelings are the deepest thing in us, and our whole culture has bought into this lie. "It can't be wrong if it feels so right" is a very convenient philosophy for addicts and tyrants.

God works most effectively in our lives when He seems most absent—as He did to Christ on the Cross ("My God, my God, why have you forsaken me?"). A little effort in such times, without the aid of feelings, brings us farther on the road to holiness, makes us more real, more solid, more tough, than much effort when aided by feelings—not because there is anything wrong with feelings, but because feelings are not free, not willed, not chosen. You can't create a feeling in yourself or in someone else simply by willing it. But you can create a free choice in yourself just by willing it. Choices come from you, feelings come to you—not from the external physical world, but from the unfree and unconscious sources within the soul. We are often "overcome" by feelings; we are never "overcome" by will. Feelings are passive, willing is active.

This is why God instituted sacraments for everyone instead of techniques for having ecstatic mystical experiences, which He gives only to a few. He hides from our feelings as well as our senses in order to test and strengthen our faith and love. And it works: under this treatment, our souls grow, invisibly and gradually, into strong, adult plants instead of frail ones that are subject to every wind. The hardest test is not the martyrdom of the body but the martyrdom of the feelings, the daily grind, the life of faith that is often without the aid of feelings (the saints call them "sensible consolations") and also without seeing with the external eyes or the internal eyes of our merely human reason (the saints call that "the dark night of the senses" and "the dark night of the reason", two parts of "the dark night of the soul").

Thus the saint is what Kierkegaard calls a "knight of faith". He slays not dragons but a more formidable foe: time, ordinariness, and boredom. Kierkegaard writes,

> People commonly travel around the world to see rivers and mountains, new stars, birds of rare plumage, queerly deformed fishes, ridiculous breeds of men—they abandon themselves to the bestial stupor which gapes at existence, and they think they have seen something. This does not interest me. But if I knew where there was such a knight

of faith, I would make a pilgrimage to him on foot, for this prodigy interests me absolutely. . . . I draw closer to him, watching his least movements to see whether there might not be visible a little heterogeneous fractional telegraphic message from the infinite. . . . I examine his figure from tip to toe . . . (but) he is solid through and through. . . . One can discover nothing of that aloof and superior nature whereby one recognizes the knight of the infinite. . . . And yet the whole earthly form he exhibits is a new creation.[3]

In other words, he is as human as Jesus. The more divine you are, the more human you can be.

---

[3] Søren Kierkegaard, *Fear and Trembling* (Chicago: Aristeus Books, 2014), 20–21.

14

Holiness Is Easy

That claim sounds simply ridiculous. Obviously it's not easy, because it's rare.

It is rare, but not because it's so hard that only the few can do it. All can do it. All are called to do it. (The "universal call" to holiness is taught by all the saints and Doctors of the Church, and by the Church's *Catechism*.) All *must* do it. ("You therefore, must be perfect, as your heavenly Father is perfect" [Mt 5:48]). Imperfect citizens cannot make up an eternally perfect Kingdom of Heaven. All *will* do it, for "God is easy to please but hard to satisfy" (George MacDonald, quoted by C. S. Lewis in *Mere Christianity* [HarperOne, 2015], p. 201). That's why there's a Purgatory.

De Caussade says, at the beginning of his book, that he wrote it to dispel the illusion and excuse that holiness is too hard for most of us: "God has compelled me to write this to help you who seek to be holy and are discouraged by what you have read in the lives of saints and some books dealing with spiritual matters." And here is why we should not be discouraged: "God, who is all goodness, has made easily available for all the things necessary for (physical) life, such as earth, air and water. . . . When we turn to spiritual matters, love and loyalty are

just as vital [to spiritual life as air and water are to physical life], so they cannot be as difficult to acquire as we
imagine" (p. 23).

The argument is logical even though the conclusion is
startling. De Caussade puts it baldly: "How easy it is to
be holy" (p. 22).

Why then aren't most people very holy? Not because
it is not easy but simply because, as William Law says,
in *A Serious Call to a Devout and Holy Life*, if we examine
ourselves with honesty we will discover only one reason
why we are not as holy as the saints: because we do not
wholly want to be.

We call that "simplistic" because we do not want it to
be true. We want excuses. But when we start looking for
excuses, we can know that the time has come to do the
thing that we are giving excuses for not doing.

You may reply: That's not fair. I do, honestly and sincerely, want to be a saint. I know it is the meaning and
end and purpose of life, the will of God, and the secret
of joy. Yet I am not a saint. Why not, if it is easy?

To such a person I say two things, each as indispensable
as the other. (So please do not choose one and neglect
the other.) The first is that you are already a saint. You
have chosen the road to holiness. You are just not very
far along it. If the desire for holiness is in you, God is in
you. And He will certainly bring you to your desired end.
"Blessed are those who hunger and thirst for righteousness, for they shall be satisfied" (Mt 5:6). "Seek, and you
will find" (Mt 7:7).

The second point is that holiness is *not* easy in the sense
of requiring little effort and sacrifice. It costs everything.

And therefore it is a battle, because Original Selfishness, with which we are all born, wars against the heart's sincere desire to give all, to love, to trust, to believe, to hope, to abandon self. We are in a spiritual war, and "the former man" (Rom 6:6) is Satan's spy in our soul, and he thrashes and screams a lot, even though he cannot win in the end. "The desires of the flesh are against the Spirit, and the desires of the Spirit are against the flesh" (Gal 5:17).

"Flesh" in Scripture does not mean "body" (those are two different Greek words, *sarx* and *soma*). And "Spirit" does not mean "soul". Those are also two different words, *pneuma* and *psyche*. "Flesh" means selfish, foolish, fallen human nature, body and soul. And "Spirit" means regenerated, "born-again" human nature, human nature inhabited by the Holy Spirit, both body and soul.

T. S. Eliot tells us both why it is easy and why it is hard in the same phrase when he calls being a Christian "a condition of complete simplicity / Costing not less than everything." (*Four Quartets*). It is easy because it is "a condition of complete simplicity". It is hard because it is "costing not less than everything".

It is easy because it is not complex. You don't have to know many things or do many things or accomplish many things or master techniques. It is not a science or a technology.

It is also easy because, though it costs everything and demands repeated sacrifice, it also supplies repeated joy. "All the way to Heaven is Heaven", said Saint Catherine of Siena. We know this by experience. Every time we choose unselfish love, every time we give ourselves away to God and neighbor, we get something back: a deep, quiet, iron-solid joy. And the more we give, the more we get. The more we unbutton the armor of the ego, the more light and life and warmth and air comes flowing into our souls from God. God Himself makes it easy by strewing the road with the peace the world cannot give. But He limits His treats so that we don't get a spiritual sweet tooth.

Every one of us is capable of such love. All the saints say this. Anyone can be a saint. Imagine all the good Hitler could have done if he had been a saint.

God's universal call to sanctity is so adamant that He will never let us enter Heaven until we have become saints, no matter what it costs in purgation, in this world and in the next, and no matter what it cost God Himself when He suffered Hell on the Cross.

"You must be perfect." Jesus never exaggerated, never lied, never did a cute little two-step dance shuffle around hard truths. Our scholars "nuance" His hard sayings, try to soften His diamonds by turning them back into coal, try to turn His wine back into water. They try to make the hard thing easier that way, but in so doing they make the easy thing hard.

15

Methods

Methods make things easier. They are means to ends. They are good if they work to attain their ends; they are not good if they don't.

But there is no method for faith, hope, or love. You just choose to do it. The choosing is the doing. Free choice does not work by methods. Methods work by the law of causality: if you supply this cause, you will get this effect. But free choice is not just another link in the chain of causes; if it were, it would not be free. Free choice creates a new chain of causes, as God creates a new universe.

But there are methods for the *aids* to holiness. For instance, schedules, like prayer five times a day. That is an excellent habit; why not copy it from the Muslims? Monks pray seven times a day. Lay people don't have that much time, but seven one-minute prayers at seven different times every day are possible and more effective than one seven-minute prayer a day. Why not take a full minute before and after each meal (since three meals a day is just about our only reliably repeated pattern to fit into) plus after waking and before retiring? Then if you miss one of those eight you still did seven.

There are methods of prayer, or at least road maps: maps for moving from verbal prayer to meditation and from meditation to contemplation. The maps are easier to understand than you may think and easier at least to begin to follow than they seem. But always KISS (Keep It Simple, Stupid). That is one of my most reliable and tested mottos.

But methods are not absolutely necessary. There is only "one thing . . . needful" (Lk 10:42). Many saints do not speak of methods or degrees at all, but all of them speak of the "one thing . . . needful". That one thing has many names. "Abandonment", "islam" (the surrender, the practice, not the institutional religion), and "faith" (trusting love) are three of them.

Holiness transcends methods (though it does not despise them and often uses them), and it also transcends words for the same reason: because it is simple. Mary was the simplest and therefore the most laconic of the saints. "Let it be to me according to your word"—that's all! *All the secrets of all the saints and mystics are there.* All of mystical theology is embodied in her. Mary's advice to us is wonderfully simple: "Do whatever he tells you" (Jn 2:5). That's all. That's everything.

How many words does it take to say that we don't need many words? As Lao Tzu says, "Knowing that enough is enough, is enough." Really, we need to say only one word: "Yes." The only thing to say No to is sin.

The wisest idea I ever had came to me (clearly from divine inspiration) one day when I was about eight. It so sticks in my memory that I remember exactly where I was: riding west on Haledon Avenue in Prospect Park, New Jersey, passing the corner of North Eighth Street, after church one Sunday morning. I had been confused by all the things I was taught in church and Sunday School, and I asked my father, "Dad, all this stuff we learn in church, it all comes down to just one thing, right?" He answered with some suspicion, "Just one thing? What do you mean?" I replied, "We just have to ask God what He wants us to do and then just do it, right?" A proud smile replaced suspicion on his face: "You're absolutely right, son."

It's been all downhill since then.

16

Faith, Hope, and Love
Are Only One Thing

De Caussade says: "The state of self-abandonment is a blending of faith, hope and love in one single act" (p. 60).

What does that look like?

Like the look a little baby gives to his Mommy or Daddy when looking up into a big, smiling face. Like the look a purring cat gives you when you stroke its fur. Like the look a dog gives you when it wags its tail. That's why God invented cats and dogs: to teach us what faith, hope, and love look like. What do we see in that look? No judgment. No reasoning. No doubts. No thoughts. No worry about tomorrow. Just love. What kind of love? Faith-hope-love.

De Caussade says these three theological virtues are "blended" in one act. It's even stronger than that: they are not just held together; they become one simple act. You say Yes to God with your whole heart and, therefore, with all three powers of your heart, the intellect (faith) and the will (love) and the desires (hope).

The great philosopher Kant once said that the three greatest human questions are: What can I know? What should I do? and What may I hope? The three theological virtues are the Christian answer to these three questions. Faith tells us the essential truth about ourselves and our relation to God; and love tells us our essential moral task; and hope tells us that our fundamental desire, the desire not just for pleasure or even for happiness, but for joy, will be fulfilled.

Although faith is primarily in the intellect, and love in the will, and hope in the feelings or emotions, yet each of these three theological virtues, faith and hope and love, has an intellectual and a volitional and an emotional component.

The intellectual component of faith is belief. Its volitional component is "the will to believe". The choice to believe combines the mind's belief and the will's command. The emotional component of faith is confidence. This can be both a cause and an effect of faith in the mind and will.

The essence of faith is trust. Trust is not merely emotional. Your bank is a "trust company" because you entrust your money to it, but you don't need to feel warm fuzzies toward your bank for it to work.

The first sin, in Eden, was unbelief in the sense of lack of trust. The Devil told Eve that God was not to be trusted. That mistrust led to every other sin.

God's remedy for our mistrust is His infinite and all-powerful mercy, which is stronger than all our sins. God's mercy makes holiness easy because it makes our basic task not hard penances but joyful trust. Our joy (in the form of trust) brings down God's joy (in the form of mercy).

Saint Faustina writes: "The graces of My mercy are drawn by means of one vessel only, and that is—trust. The more a soul trusts, the more it will receive."

Hope's intellectual component is belief that God will fulfill all His promises. Its volitional component is the choice to believe that and the choice to hold despair at bay. Its emotional component is joy, which naturally results from the belief that God will give us all good.

Love's intellectual component is knowledge of the object loved and of its (or his or her) lovability and worth and value and beauty. Its volitional component is the choice to love, which is its essence. Its emotional component is compassion.

There is an order: the will cannot will unless the intellect sees and specifies the object willed. You can't love what you don't know. (Do you love "quomth"?)

The emotional components are results of the intellectual and volitional components. They are gifts of God, designed for us and attached to the virtues. But even when these emotional gifts are temporarily withheld, to test and strengthen our faith and hope and love, the substance of our faith and hope and love can still be fully present.

Hope is really the same thing as faith; it is faith directed to the future. It therefore shares many of the attributes of faith. Like faith, it includes trust in the wisdom of God, who always knows what is best for us, and in the love of God, which always wills what is best for us, and in the power of God, which always accomplishes what it wills.

But love is simpler than faith and hope. You can say that faith and hope mean this or that, but you can only say that love means love. It cannot be defined by anything simpler. It is like the number one.

Faith, hope, and love are like the body, soul, and spirit of a person: you can't have one without the other two. A body without a soul is a corpse, and a human soul without a spirit is a spiritual corpse. Souls can die, by the loss of their spirits, just as bodies can die by the loss of their souls. Gogol wrote a story called *Dead Souls*. You can see them walking the streets of any of our cities. They look like what they are: zombies. They are scarier than the fictional kind.

Faith, hope, and love are one virtue or one attitude in a way analogous to the way in which the visible body and the invisible soul are one human person, or the way in which the divine nature and the human nature of Christ are one Divine Person, or the way in which our free will and God's predestination are one historical event, or the way in which a husband and wife are one flesh.

All of these analogies transcend mathematics and the clear, analytical either/or logic that is like mathematics. That is why they are "mysteries". When we analyze out different components of them, one at a time, it is like a doctor putting a sheet over the body of the person on whom he is operating and cutting a hole in it so that he can operate through the hole and focus on only that one of the many organs in the body. The organ does not and cannot live alone. If you cut it out of the body, it dies. That is why "faith by itself, if it has no works [the works of love], is dead" (Jas 2:17).

17

Unselfconsciousness

De Caussade says: "You seek your own idea of God, although you have him in his reality" (p. 94). Which would you prefer? It is the difference between Heaven and Hell.

For Hell is pure ego, pure self-consciousness. I do not believe there is physical fire in Hell; I believe this is intended as a symbol. For if there were physical fire in Hell, it would distract us out of our deeper pain. Spiritual pain is deeper, and worse, than physical pain; and we often unconsciously recognize this when we are in such spiritual pain that we deliberately distract ourselves from it by tearing our hair out or banging our head against a wall.

Fire is beautiful, and there is nothing beautiful in Hell.

In Hell, my will is always done, because there is nothing else there but my will. There is no Other. The otherness that goes all the way up into the eternal divine life of the Trinity and is the source of its joy is totally extinguished. At the opposite pole from self-conscious self-love, we find the ecstasy, the "standing-outside-self" (that's the literal meaning of "ecstasy"), of unselfconscious other-love.

That is why masturbation is bad: it substitutes subjectivity for objectivity, self for other. God designed sex to bring us out of ourselves, not into ourselves; out of our "my will be done." Love is supposed to bring us out of the dark prison of the "my will be done" ego into the joys of "thy will be done", both horizontally and vertically, toward both the human and the divine Other. But self-love turns it back on itself. Masturbation is the physical, sexual form of self-love.

C. S. Lewis says:

> For me the real evil of masturbation [would] be that it takes an appetite which, in lawful use, leads the individual out of himself to complete (and correct) his own personality in that of another (and finally in children and even grandchildren) and turns it back: sends the man back into the prison of himself, there to keep a harem of imaginary brides. And this harem, once admitted, works against his *ever* getting out and really uniting with a real woman. For the harem is always accessible, always subservient, calls for no sacrifices or adjustments, and can be endowed with erotic and psychological attractions which no real woman can rival. Among those shadowy brides he is always adored, always the perfect lover: no demand is made on his unselfishness, no mortification ever imposed on his vanity. In the end, they become merely the medium through which he increasingly adores himself. . . . After all, almost the *main* work of life is to *come out* of our selves, out of the little, dark prison we are all born in. Masturbation is to be avoided as *all* things are to be avoided [which] retard this process. The danger is that of coming to *love* the prison.[1]

All the "peak experiences" of our lives are unselfconscious. All mystical experiences are unselfconscious—so

---

[1] *The Collected Letters of C. S. Lewis* (New York: HarperCollins, 2007), 758–59.

much so that many mystics become pantheists, because they don't see themselves any more, just God.

We are destined for ecstasy. (The word means, literally, "standing-outside-yourself".) That is why we become addicted to substitutes: drugs, alcohol, sex. Pleasure is not enough. Even happiness is not enough: it gets boring. Nothing less than joy will do. That is why Scripture lists joy as one of the fruits of the Spirit, but not happiness or pleasure.

Sometimes joy is striking. Sometimes it is quiet. But it is never boring.

Holiness, and its attendant joy, usually comes gradually. De Caussade says: "Perfection . . . begins, grows, and comes to fruition in our souls so secretly that we are not aware of it" (p. 24).

It is like the growth of the body. When we grow physically, we grow without awareness of it. When we grow spiritually, when we grow in holiness, we also grow without awareness of it. In another sense, this growth is not like the growth of the body because it happens only by effort, will, and choice. But both growths are gradual and secret and unconscious. If either growth were conscious, we would spoil it: we would try to control it, technologize it, micromanage it; we'd try to my-will-be-done it. That is dangerous with physical growth and impossible with growth in holiness, because the very essence of holiness is "*Thy* will be done."

"Thy will be done" is what faith, hope, and love look like. That is also the secret of joy.

18

"Love Is All You Need"

It is true that love is all you need. That is not true of any partial kind of love. But it is profoundly true of the love that God is. (Notice that I said "the love that God is", not "the love that is God". "God is love" but love is not God.)

As oranges are the fruit of orange trees, love is the fruit of faith and hope; and therefore love involves the whole plant, roots and shoots and fruits together.

De Caussade says that "the whole business of self-abandonment is only the business of loving" (p. 111) Once again, it is totally simple. As Kierkegaard says in his lovely book title, "purity of heart is to will one thing."

~

Saint Thomas says that love has two forms: desiring the good when absent and rejoicing in it when present. *Agapē*, and therefore holiness, is the one and only desire that is granted infallible fulfillment. "Seek and you shall find" does not refer to anything else: long life, conquest of earthly enemies, freedom from pain, disease, death, betrayal, weakness, and so on. But it does refer to God and to that which God is: "God is *agapē*." That is why all who seek it find it. De Caussade says: "If you search for this kingdom where God alone rules, you can be quite sure you will find it" (p. 112). For you find it in the very act of seeking it, loving it. The more you seek it, the more you love it, the more you will find it. For "the moment we long for God and [long] to obey his will, we enjoy him . . . the fullness of our enjoyment exactly matches the extent of our desire for him" (p. 112).

To "enjoy" here means really to have it, not necessarily to feel it. God *is* our joy. But we can have God without feeling joy, and we can also feel joy without really having God. It can be false joy. Would you rather feel it and not have it and be deceived or have it although you do not feel it? Is feeling more important than being? Is a deceived but satisfied consciousness what you want?

Love is indeed all you need because God is love and God is all you need. If God is not all you need, then God is not God but only a finite part of a greater whole.

If God is not love, we have no hope.

This is another reason why holiness is so simple: it is only love. "Let others, Lord, ask you for all sorts of gifts. Let them increase their prayers and entreaties. But I, my Lord, ask for one thing only and have only a single prayer —give me a pure heart" (p. 66).

Why is this right?

1. Because your heart is your self, and if your heart is black and dead, you are black and dead, while if your heart is full of light and life, then you are, too. "If then the light in you is darkness, how great is the darkness!" (Mt 6:23).

2. And because only God can give you a new heart.

3. And because deep down you know that you need a heart transplant. That's why you have to die: death is anesthesia. Before death anesthetizes us, we keep jumping about on the operating table telling the divine Surgeon what to do.

4. And because you know you need this purity, singleness, simpleness, oneness of heart. All sins come from divided hearts.

5. And because this is what God wants for you: perfection. Love is never satisfied with anything less. The Lover must say to the beloved: "You are all fair, my love; there is no flaw in you" (Song 4:7). This is what the divine bridegroom says to the human bride, not just vice versa, in the Song of Songs!

Love (*agapē*) continues to love the beloved even when she is less than fair, when she is disfigured by sin, but in spite of her disfigurement, not because of it. And love cannot not will its removal. And complete love cannot not will its complete removal.

Augustine says, "amor meus, pondus meum", my love is my weight, my gravity. I go where my love goes. I become what I love. My love is my destiny. Therefore, if my love is divided, my destiny and my joy and my very identity are divided. Only one great love can make one great person.

That is why God allows us to suffer. For only the heart that is broken by love can be a whole heart. The heart is an egg: it is designed to crack and hatch. The only alternative is not comfortable selfishness; it is rottenness. There is in the end no such thing as comfortable selfishness. That is a rich world's most dangerous illusion.

19

Love and Sex

When we think of love, we think of sex. This is not wrong, because it is natural, since sex is the most passionate form of natural love. And it is not wrong, also, because it is also supernatural. Sex is supernatural because sex is the biological image of the image of God.

This is not a new idea but a very old one. The very first time "the image of God" is mentioned in the Bible (Gen 1:27) "the image of God" is identified as "male and female". The reason for this is that God is love, and love is a relationship between persons; that is why, in Christian theology, the one God is not just one person but three: Lover, Beloved, and Loving.

"The sacrament of the present moment", as de Caussade calls it, is spiritual sex. It is our tryst with God our Lover. Because of this, "every moment of our lives can be a kind of communion with his love" (p. 46). Every moment God's holy will asks you for your response, and each time you say Yes, your soul becomes pregnant with His life. Holiness is sexy. That is why sex is holy.

You say this sexual image for holiness is not a good one. You are right, but for the opposite reason than you think. Sex is not too passionate an image, too strong; it is too weak, it is not passionate enough. The ecstasy of the flesh is such a pale and inadequate image of the ecstasy of the spirit that it is comical.

Therefore our asking "Can you have sex in Heaven?" is like a small child asking "Can you eat chocolates while you have sex?" (The analogy is from C. S. Lewis.) It is like asking: "Can I find a drop of water in the ocean?" or "Can I find any warmth in the sun?"

20

When to Find God:
"The Sacrament of the Present Moment"

Why does de Caussade call the present moment a sacrament?

Because it is holy and can make us holy.

In fact, only the present moment can make us holy. The past cannot, because it is dead, and the future cannot, because it is not yet born.

Twist and turn as you will, you cannot be, you cannot live, you cannot act, anywhen except in the present moment. You are always confined to that one time just as you are always confined to the one place of your body. You cannot escape your skin.

Of course you can have out-of-body experiences, both preternatural (unusual ones we hear about from people at the brink of death) and natural ones (reading a novel that takes your mind out of your body and makes you identify with the characters and places and times in the novel rather than with the world your body is inhabiting as you are reading it). And because you are a human being rather than an animal, you can consciously and deliberately remember the past, and anticipate the future with planning, desire, or fear. But only in the present can you remember the past or anticipate the future. You can do nothing in the past (although you can do something *about* the past: you can remember it, you can forget it, you can understand it, you can misunderstand it). But there is no past you: it is dead. And there is no future you: it has not yet come into existence. You can only do something *about* the future: you can worry about it, or you can plan it responsibly, and you can trust God with it. The object of your consciousness may well be the past or the future, but the subject of your consciousness is always present.

Yet we usually live in the two unreal times. We think about the past and the future much more than we should and about the present much less than we should. We let the past and future control us. Because someone did something to us in the past, we still carry around its wounds with us in the present. That is unavoidable physically, but it is not unavoidable mentally. There is a key out of the prison of the past, and it is called forgiveness. Jesus used it on the Cross to forgive the good thief. While everyone else was living in the past and rejoicing that the thief was getting what his past sins deserved, Jesus lived in the present ("today") and saw, in that present moment, Paradise in the heart of the repentant thief. That's why he said to him: "Today you will be with me in Paradise" (Lk 23:43). The only reason the thief would enter Paradise a few hours later, when he died, is because he was in Paradise already in his repentant heart. Jesus, the perfect psychologist, saw that and pronounced it. Repentance and forgiveness worked like a two-part key, like the key to a safe deposit box (neither part can work without the other) to liberate the good thief from his past.

We also let the future control us by living in desire.

Buddha perceived that and counseled the desperate psycho-therapy of a total abolition of desire, a spiritual euthanasia, killing the patient to cure the disease of suffering that, Buddha rightly saw, was the inevitable consequence of living in the future and identifying, not with what actually exists in the present, but with what we desire to exist in the future. He saw that suffering was the gap between desire and satisfaction, and since it is impossible to increase satisfaction to the level of desire, he counseled decreasing desire to the level of satisfaction. And even farther, to zero. For even if we are totally content and satisfied, we still desire that satisfaction to continue into the future, thus we still live in the future and in desire and, therefore, in fear. Whether you are poor and desire a million dollars or rich and have it, you fear the future; for in the first case you fear the future that is as poor as the present, and in the second case you fear the future that is more poor than the present.

Jesus does not agree with Buddha's radical prescription, a desire-ectomy. But he does agree with Buddha's diagnosis. Selfish desire, egotism, greed, "my will be done", is indeed the cause of suffering. Jesus and Buddha agree that we need a "new birth", a radical spiritual surgery. But Jesus' prescription is to convert desire rather than to kill it; to change its quality (from selfish to unselfish) and its object (God's will, not our own); and to desire with *more* passion, not less, when we desire God's will rather than our own, since that will, unlike ours, is perfect (omniscient, omnipotent, and omnibenevolent). Thus we can live in Romans 8:28.

Hope does not contradict this principle of living in the present. Hope lives in the present, not in the future, by refusing to worry about it because hope puts its whole future in the perfect hands of God, where it belongs, and leaves it there, rather than picking at it like a teenager picking at his pimples. By your present faith in the omniscience, omnipotence, and omnibenevolence of the God who lives and acts in the present, you are freed from worry about the future. You can be just as certain that God will give you little pieces of Heaven, little appetizers for Heaven, for the rest of your life on earth as you can be certain that He will give you the fullness of Heaven when you die. You can be as free from temporal worry about losing temporal goods before you die as you can be free from eternal worry about losing eternal goods after you die. For God has saved you; and your salvation includes the salvation of your whole life on earth, in time, including its whole past and future. What he did for the repentant thief, he will do for you.

Buddha argued that desire always causes suffering because it creates a gap between what you have and what you want. So he counseled the abolition of all desire. But hope is not a desire. It is almost the opposite of desire, since its object is not something in the future but something in the present: not the good things you want God to give you in the future but the good God who is giving you exactly what you need in the present.

~

If you want to meet God, you have to go where He is *and when He is*. And "when He is" is the present moment.

What about "where He is"? You don't have to move from where you are to go to Him; because He is everywhere, and therefore He is right where you are. And you do not so much go to Him, as He comes to you; He takes the initiative. And He comes to you where you are, where you are real. If you are in Boston, He does not come to New York but to Boston. The only places He does not come to are places where you are not, for instance, places about which you only fantasize. If you are in Detroit dreaming you are in Hawaii, He does not come to you in Hawaii: He comes to you in Detroit.

The same is true of time as is true of space: He comes to us only when we are as well as where we are, and we are only in the "when" of the present moment. We are alive only in the present. "Now is the day of salvation" (2 Cor 6:2).

He is knocking right now, at this exact present moment, at the door of your life, of your life's time; and that door is the present moment. Open the door of your heart and your life to Him now. (The door to your life *is* your heart.) Now! Not tomorrow. Tomorrow is always a day away.

Tomorrow is what today always is in Hell. Since "Now is the day of salvation", there is no Now in Hell because there is no salvation in Hell.

Only in the present can you act. Only in the present can you choose to open the prison gates of past and future. Only in the present can you change your future, and even the meaning of your past, as the Good Thief did. Only in the present can you meet God. Only in the present can you be holy.

Planning to be holy is not being holy. Fantasizing about being holy is not being holy. People with active minds and imaginations can deceive themselves into subconsciously thinking they are holy just because they dream of being holy, because people with active minds and imaginations sometimes find more life, more reality, in what they think and dream than in what they actually live.

This is a malady that affects mainly "thinkers" and "dreamers". Ordinary people are anchored more securely to the real world. Insanity is more frequent among philosophers than among farmers. That's why we have a saying in academia: "That idea is so insane you have to have a PhD to believe it." Of course, active minds and imaginations are good things and gifts of God; but all gifts can be misused. And we are all very, very clever at inventing ways to misuse them.

Bottom line: If this is all true (and you know it is), then just give yourself, your whole self, to God right now, at this present moment, irrevocably and completely and forever. For there is no other time than right now to do it.

No, don't just read about it. Don't go from paragraph to paragraph like a hamster on a wheel. Stop the wheel and get off. Enter eternity by dealing, at this present moment, with the eternal and therefore present God right now.

In other words, in a single word, pray.

21

The Future

Of course we need to plan for the future, especially the immediate future (you're doing that now when reading this sentence) and the ultimate future (Heaven). Once we have given up the habit of worrying about the future and have entrusted it to God, we can let it come back into our mind without claws that tear us apart emotionally with worry.

God has told us the most important thing we can possibly know about our future. He has not told us the details of our future either on earth or in Heaven. (Scripture describes Heaven mainly symbolically.) Instead, He has told us something infinitely more important than that. He has not told us *what* it is but He has told us *where* it is: it is in His hand. And He has told us that therefore "all things work together for good" for us. And therefore He told Lady Julian of Norwich that "all shall be well, and all shall be well, and all manner of thing shall be well." De Caussade says: "All will be well. God has the matter in hand. We need fear nothing" (p. 99). Those three short sentences tell us (1) the good news, (2) its reason, and (3) its consequence. Repeat his words to yourself every day. Ask yourself: Do I really believe that? If your answer is "Yes, I do, but my faith is fragile and weak", then pray

"Lord, I believe, help my unbelief!" (cf. Mk 9:24). And keep praying it until you die.

Because our faith is real, "we need fear nothing." But because our faith is weak, we do continue to fear, even though we do not need to. So what? Let the fear come. That, too, is part of God's perfect plan. De Caussade says: "Our very fear and sense of desolation are verses in this hymn of darkness. We delight in singing every syllable of them, knowing that all ends with 'Glory be to the Father'" (p. 99).

God is presently weaving a tapestry. (The image comes from Thornton Wilder's *The Bridge of San Luis Rey*.) It is a masterpiece. It is our lives. We see only the loose threads on the back side of it. Only He sees it as it is. In Heaven, we will see it as He does. On earth, we can only believe it. And how can we not believe it, when He Himself assures us of it? Romans 8:28 is divine revelation, not human rationalization.

Wilder probably got his image from de Caussade, who says: "God's achievement [in our lives] is like the front of a lovely tapestry. . . . [We] see only the back as he adds stitch after stitch with his needle, yet all these stitches are slowly creating a magnificent picture which appears in all its glory only when every stitch is done and it is viewed from the right side. But all this beauty cannot be seen as it is being created" (p. 102).

Many other saints, mystics, and poets say the same startling thing. Thomas Traherne says that "the world is a mirror of infinite beauty, yet no one sees it" (Meditation 31). Dostoyevsky says, "We are all in paradise, but we don't want to realize it, and if we did care to realize it,

paradise would be established in all the world tomorrow"
(*Brothers Karamazov*).

This is not just a beautiful idea or ideal. It has life-changing practical consequences. De Caussade tells us that "the self-abandoned soul . . . sees only God and its duty. To fulfill this duty moment by moment consists in adding tiny stitches to the work; yet it is by these stitches that God accomplishes those marvels of which we sometimes catch a glimpse now, but which will not be known truly until the great day of eternity" (p. 102).

De Caussade uses another image, the master chess player: "When it comes to the moment of our death, the Holy Spirit, who secretly moves all the pieces on the board of life by his continual and fruitful activity, will say: 'Let there be light.' Then we shall behold all the riches which faith alone knew were hidden [in the puzzling moves of divine providence on the chessboard of our lives]" (p. 115).

De Caussade uses still another image from human art for this divine art: God is like a novelist, writing a great book, and we are the characters. The novelist moves his characters both into and out of troubles—otherwise, there is no story! De Caussade says, "God disentangles them from their troubles far more easily than novelists . . . extricate their heroes from all their dangers and bring them to a happy and successful end. With far greater skill and most happily does God lead them through deadly perils . . . and transforms them into the heroes of stories far stranger and more lovely than any invented by the stunted imaginings of men" (p. 110).

We, if we are holy [regenerated, saved, born again, bap-
tized], are the paper, our sufferings and our actions are
the ink. The workings of the Holy Spirit are his pen, and
with it he writes a living gospel. But it will never be read
until that last day of glory when it leaves the printing
press of this life. And what a splendid book it will be—
the book the Holy Spirit is still writing! . . . Never a day
passes when type is not set, ink applied and pages pulled
. . . we shall be able to read it only in heaven. . . . What
now seems to me so confused, so incoherent, so foolish
and so fanciful will then delight and entrance me by its
order, its beauty, its wisdom. (p. 93)

"I wonder what kind of a story we're in", Sam muses
to Frodo as they trek across the bleak, hopeless landscape
of Mordor in *The Lord of the Rings*. We are more blessed
than Frodo and Sam, because they could only intuit and
hope; they could only respond to the deep but obscure
suggestions that God inscribes in every human heart; but
we can believe and know what God has told us, by infallible (how could God goof?) divine revelation, of the
answer to that question, which is the most important of
all questions because it is the question of "What is the
meaning of life?"

22

Peace

Restlessness and rest, war and peace, are both our lot here.

Because He has made us for Himself, therefore our hearts are restless until they rest in Him. (That sentence from Augustine's *Confessions* is the most beloved and most quoted of all sentences written by Christians outside of Scripture.)

There are three stages of life. The first is restlessness, the restlessness of the heart that has not yet found God, the heart of Augustine before his conversion. The second is the stage of post-conversion peace, the peace the world cannot give, the peace of Romans 8:28. But this is also a stage of war, because the plot of the story is still being written, and there are still enemies attacking us, and our fighting is still full of weaknesses and defeats, sins and sorrows, follies and fantasies. It is a mixture of lights and darknesses, like the plot of any story. The third stage is the perfect Heavenly peace.

Both in the imperfect second stage (earth) and in the perfect third stage (Heaven), de Caussade says "we cannot enjoy true peace unless we submit to God's will" (p. 29). That is the supreme rule of all stages. T. S. Eliot says that the most profound line in literature is Dante's "In His will is our peace."

"Peace" and "surrender" are the two meanings of the word "islam". It is cognate to the Hebrew "shalom". (Notice the same consonant progression: s-l-m.)

In the present struggle, the restlessness of our hearts is the second greatest blessing in our lives. It is a greater blessing than any false peace. The only greater blessing is the true peace that comes from God, the peace that alone quiets this restlessness, and does so both imperfectly and intermittently in this life and perfectly and eternally in Heaven. That restlessness is blessed because it is the restlessness of which Jesus spoke in the beatitude: "Blessed are those who hunger and thirst for [perfect] righteousness [holiness], for they shall be satisfied" (Mt 5:6).

So if the reason you bought this book was the title ("holiness"), and if you seek that holiness in your heart, then you will certainly attain your desire. If not, Jesus is a fool or a liar.

23

Failures

We will fail. All of us sinners fail. We *have* to fail. If we did not fail, we would have no hope. We would be totally successful and self-satisfied and proud in our selfishness and sinfulness and willfulness. Our very failures are a necessary part of God's perfect plan for us, part of Romans 8:28. All our failures, except one, are part of His perfect plan and, therefore, part of our perfect success. The only failure that is not is the final refusal of God's love and mercy.

There are three kinds of failures: (1) physical sufferings (pains, diseases, deaths, catastrophes), (2) internal weaknesses (including personal mental and emotional weaknesses), and (3) sins.

Here is why there are three categories, not just one or two. (1) Sufferings come to us, not from us; they come against our will, not by our will. We are passive to them. (3) Sins come from us, not to us, by our will, not against it. We actively choose to sin. (The more we struggle with the good part of our will against the sins that come from the bad part of our will, the less responsible we are for our sins. That is why the cold sins of the spirit are more terrible than the hot sins of the flesh that come from weaknesses that are struggled against.) (2) The middle category, emotional and mental problems, are neither wholly passive (like physical sufferings) nor wholly active (like sins), but mixed. They come from within, but from our subconscious mind and feelings rather than from our deliberate, free choice. They are not sins, and we are not responsible for them. (However, we are responsible for deliberately encouraging bad feelings, which in turn lead to sinful acts, for example, by using pornography.) That is why homosexual desires, or same-sex attraction, is not a sin, but same-sex acts ("sodomy") are, just as adulterous heterosexual desires are not sins, but adulterous heterosexual acts are. Homosexuals and heterosexuals do not have different moral rules. (All this is knowable, if we are totally honest with ourselves, by common sense, honesty, and reason. It does not depend on any particular religion.)

The first and second kinds of failure (pains and weaknesses, from without or from within) are both to be endured and accepted in faith when they cannot be overcome and avoided. Only the third kind of failures, moral failures, sins, are to be hated and not accepted, for they alone do not come from God in any way.

1. Good things come from God directly. He invented them and directly wills them, because He loves us and lovers always want their beloved to be happy, as happy as possible, as truly happy, deeply happy, long-range happy as possible, even if that requires temporary unhappiness. God wills the removal of these physical blessings only when He knows that this removal would work for our greater good. That includes physical weakness, old age, disease, and death, all of which came about because of the Fall but which God uses for good. As the Wisdom of Sirach says, "God did not make death" (Wis 1:13); but He uses it as our door to eternal life.

2. Our internal, spiritual, and mental and emotional weaknesses and sufferings, which are also results of the Fall, are also permitted by God and used for our greater good. He wills both our physical and emotional sufferings indirectly, not for their own sakes, but for the sake of the greater good and greater happiness that they produce in us.

3. Only our sins are not willed by God, because they are not for our good or our benefit. Only our repentance and turning from them is for our good. God foreknows and permits our sins, but only to preserve our free will (love does not want perfect robots) and to head us off from pride, the most dangerous sin of all.

What is true of death is true of all the little deaths that precede it. God is preparing us for a far greater life, a greater happiness. He takes our toys from us when it is time to grow up and play with the jewels of truth and goodness and beauty. He takes our comforts from us when it is time to grow up and learn to forget ourselves and our comforts and to find far deeper joy in loving other people and to find far greater joy in that than we could ever find in our own comforts. He takes from us our very hearts' desires so that we can give our hearts away, for giving away your heart is the only way to find it. The only whole heart is one that has been first broken and then healed. He takes from us all the things we love so that we can love Him alone and then get all our other loves back, transformed and perfected, in the only form in which they can ever be ours forever. He thwarts our dalliances so that we can give ourselves to Him in marriage. He takes us away from our cottage so that we can live in His castle. He takes us away from our dying cinders (we are all Cinderella) so that we can live in His living fire.

God wills us not only to suffer things that come to our person from without but also things that come to our lives from weaknesses within our own personalities, for example, being shy, afraid of pain, slow-witted about some things, like math or what to say at parties or how to "read between the lines" or unable to enjoy sports or animals or the sea or other perfectly good things. God did not make us perfect. Everyone has something at which they are very bad and something at which they are very good. That is part of individuality. That involves real defects in our personalities—defects, but not sins. We are invited to stop beating ourselves up about them and to entrust them to God, who knows exactly what He is doing. De Caussade says: "Let us benefit by our weaknesses and failures, our fears and doubts: let us draw good from our infirmities" (p. 89).

De Caussade puts external sufferings, failures, and weaknesses in exactly the same boat when he says: "It is in order to stimulate and sustain this faith that God allows the soul to be buffeted and swept away by the raging torrent of so much distress, so many troubles, so much embarrassment and weakness, and so many setbacks" (p. 93). As in a great novel, the hero's failures are part of his success because success is a "success *story*". And the theme of the story is Romans 8:28. That story is far more exciting than Utopia. That's why God let the snake into Eden.

What of sins? What of moral failures? Couldn't God give us the grace to overcome more sins? Of course He could. Why doesn't He, then? God does not will them, but He permits them, both to preserve our free will and to humble our pride. If we overcame all other sins, we would succumb to pride and our last state would be far worse than our first. We would be super-Pharisees.

So if you want to overcome some other sin, start with pride. If you want to grow some missing virtue, start with humility.

24

Suffering

A conversation overheard between two lonely people in their thirties, one married and one unmarried, went like this. The unmarried person confessed that she had never found anyone who really, deeply understood her and whom she could trust completely. All her married friends were divorced or on the verge of divorce or unhappily married. She did not think she would ever marry and had reconciled herself to a life of loneliness. Her married friend sympathized with her but said that she would gladly exchange situations with her. She was equally lonely, but married.

(Both were believing Catholics and therefore did not believe in divorce. Catholicism does not forbid divorce; it denies its existence. Unlike other churches, it does not claim to have the authority to contradict the explicit teaching of Jesus in the Gospels: Matthew 5:31–32, Matthew 19:3–12; Mark 10:4; Luke 16:18.)

Another overheard conversation was with three men sharing another common problem: each had to live with a constantly annoying person. For one, it was his boss, who was arrogant, unfair, and abusive. For another, it was his wife, who was the same. For the third, it was his semi-senile mother, who had no other living options.

Not everyone has a life that bad. But many do—far more than in past generations. (This is what we call "progress".)

It is crucial to know that this is God's love in disguise; that this suffering means not that you are less loved by God, or judged to be less worthy, but more. Those who do not suffer should worry that they are being judged by God to be unworthy of this gift or incapable of rightly using it. And the suffering that comes from other people is perhaps the deepest suffering of all.

To say that sufferings and troubles are a blessing in disguise is not, of course, to say that we should go out looking for trouble. Like death, suffering will come; as with death, we should not hasten it; and as with death, we should use it rightly and heroically.

Bottom line: the only one who can make us happy is the God who makes us suffer. It is a package deal; we must take the bitter with the sweet. He sees that they are inseparable; that sweet without bitter becomes supremely bitter in the end, and sweet with bitter becomes supremely sweet in the end.

So weep. For the same divine doctor who prescribed tears will also provide the tissues to dry your eyes. He does not say to us, and we should not say to each other, "Don't cry; everything is OK." For that's a lie. He says, "Weep. There are things to weep over. If you don't weep, you're not completely human. But remember, in your weeping, that those tears are precious jewels. Offer them up to Me in faith."

Romans 8:28 is not Pollyanna optimism or Peter Pantheism. It is not the false gospel of prosperity and happiness. That is not what the New Testament or the Torah or the Qur'an teach. They all say that suffering is necessary; it is our appointed way; it is our war.

Romans 8:28 is hope, not optimism. Optimism is a feeling: hope is a certainty. Optimism is a feeling and a prediction about the future; hope is a choice about the present presence of the God who makes suffering a present, a gift. (Notice the profound unity of the three different meanings of the word "present" there!)

Jesus did not say, in the Beatitudes, that we should be *happy* when we are poor or persecuted or hungry. He said we are *blessed*. Blessedness includes suffering because suffering is a blessing. Suffering is a blessing because it is God's gift, and all God's gifts are our blessings.

How can suffering be our blessing? It's very simple: Suffering is blessed because it brings us closer to Him.

~

Not everything in life is pleasant, and not everything in life is painful, but everything in life is providential. When we abandon ourselves to divine providence, we do not abandon ourselves only to its pleasures or only to its pains but to both. He says "Be!" to everything that is, from the light of the Big Bang to the spin of each atom, from the fall of Rome to the fall of each sparrow and the fall of each hair from our head, from the torture and crucifixion of His beloved Son to the fall and failure of our little plans and desires. And we should say "Be!" to it, too, if we want to live in reality—if reality is defined by the omniscient and omnipotent and omnibenevolent God rather than by foolish and weak and selfish us.

One more quotation from de Caussade about the "why" of suffering: "No matter what it is we attach ourselves to, God will step in and upset our plans" (p. 72). In other words, "if you want to give God a good laugh, tell Him your plans." "Attach ourselves to" means something stronger than "desire" or "care about". It is right for us to desire good things, especially good spiritual things—blessed are those who hunger and thirst after righteousness—and it is right for us to care about people. But to attach your very identity and hope and destiny to something other than God is to entrust your identity and hope and destiny to it, and that is idolatry and an infallible recipe for destruction. All idols break. Don't put divine burdens on human shoulders. God takes away our idolatries precisely to save us from that.

So when we suffer, God is lovingly slapping our hands empty and making room for Himself there, so that our hands do not make fists and close upon toys and thus close our hearts to Him. Like death, suffering is "a severe mercy" (to quote the profound title of a heartbreakingly beautiful book by Sheldon Vanauken). Death is, as de Caussade says, "God's loving strictness" (p. 73).

Those two words go together—"severe" and "mercy", "loving" and "strictness". They do not contradict each other. God's strictness, as distinct from ours, proceeds only from love, not from fear or desperation or desire for power or even justice. Lovers have surpassed justice; lovers never talk about justice or rights. Those whose hearts are set on something less than justice confuse this with looseness, but those whose hearts are set on something more than justice never do.

~

Most of our worst sufferings come from relationships with other people. Most of our greatest joys do, too. Because people have faults and weaknesses—everyone does, especially any idiot who thinks he doesn't—we must (1) accept this as a fact of life—the machine called the human psyche doesn't work perfectly. And (2) the most important thing to do about this is to remember that we are almost always causing others sufferings just as much as they are causing us to suffer. (3) So stop judging and just love.

25

Objection: I Can't Be a Saint

At this point in this book (probably long before this point), the reader is probably thinking something like this: These are beautiful ideas, but I can't live them, I can't do this, I can't be a saint.

God says you can. In fact, He says you must: "You . . . must be perfect, as your heavenly Father is perfect."

But I'm just not a Holy Joe or Holy Jane type.

There is no such type. There's only one type of human being. We're all sinners.

Right, and I'm not good enough to be a saint.

Of course you're not. That's exactly why you need to change.

But I can't do this stuff. Especially the stuff about accepting sufferings and failures.

Why not?

Because I'm not a saint. Saints can do this stuff, I can't.

You have it backward: saints don't do this stuff because they're saints; they became saints because they did this stuff.

I'm too far away from where they are.

You mean you're a rank beginner.

Right.

And therefore—do you see what follows from that correct assessment of where you are in relation to where the great saints are? Do you see what you have to do because you are such a rank beginner?

What?

You have to begin.

The task is too intimidating.

No, it isn't. In fact, you have already begun. That's why you're reading this book. If you had no interest in becoming holy, you certainly would not be reading this far.

But my beginning is so little! I've traveled an inch on a million-mile journey.

And you know what follows from that, don't you?

Hmph.

That inch makes a big difference, you know. In fact a bigger difference than any other inch of the million-mile journey.

Why?

Because it's the first inch. "Well begun is half done." You've begun. You're already on the road.

I am?

Of course you are.

Prove it to me.

Easy. Suppose you were not. Suppose you believed what you said: that you couldn't be a saint, ever. Do you see the consequences of that? Do you see what logically follows from that?

What do you mean?

That your failures have no meaning. That you have no hope.

Oh.

And that God made a mistake when He created you and called you to become a saint.

Oops.

Good Short Act of Contrition!

But . . .

You do have a big butt. Can we move it now instead of sitting on it?

So you're asking me to do high jumps with this big butt of mine?

Not at all. Notice I did not even mention contemplative prayer (yet) or heroic sacrifices.

Good. Because I'm not the next Mother Teresa.

God does not expect you to move to Calcutta.

What are you—what is He asking of me, then?

Merely to do what you are already doing: your ordinary daily duties, for God's sake.

Oh.

So to that topic let us now turn.

26

Duties

It's not a bad word. It should not connote either "doo doo" or the Nazi war criminals' excuse for cruelty and murder. ("We were only doing our duty!") It simply means what we have to do, what we have to care about: our work, our task, our job, our meaning, our reason for being in the story we are in. For most of us, it's just being a good and faithful friend, father, mother, daughter, son, brother, sister, employer, or employee.

De Caussade makes this matter of duty very simple, too, as he makes everything simple: "We have two duties to fulfill: we must actively seek to carry God's will into effect and passively accept all that his will sends us" (p. 73). That's all. That's it.

I add only two small fraternal corrections to the wording, corrections that I know de Caussade would accept. First, God's will is always effective, and our job is not to effect it, that is, to be "successful", but to be faithful, that is, obedient. Second, our "abandonment" is not passive, not a "passivity", but an active, freely chosen receptivity, like a catcher catching whatever pitch the pitcher throws to him or like a wife's acceptance of her husband's sexual love into her body.

Receiving is an activity. Mary's "Let it be to me according to your word" was the most active act in human history. She was so active in catching the ball God threw at her that she became the greatest woman in history. Because the ball God threw at her was Himself. And in a different way, a less physical way, but a real way, all of us have to be Mary: we all have to be catchers, have to catch whatever ball of Himself God throws at us. Because every time God sends us something, every time God wills something for us, that thing is, in a sense, His will, and therefore, in a sense, Himself. He's throwing us a ball of Himself every moment. That's why de Caussade calls the present moment a "sacrament".

27

Activity and Receptivity

Half of everyone's life, men and women alike, is yin, anima, feminine, receptive; and the other half is yang, animus, masculine, active; and both are equally parts of God's providence and our "abandonment" to it.

Since activity and receptivity are the two halves of our nature, of our love, and of our holiness, therefore two errors are possible: Martha-like activism that devalues contemplation and receptivity, and passive quietism that devalues action.

Quietism was a more common heresy in de Caussade's day than in ours. He writes against it: "It is a waste of time to try to picture any kind of self-abandonment which excludes all personal activity and seeks only quiescence, for if God wishes us to act for ourselves, then action makes us holy" (p. 30). What makes both activity and receptivity good is God's will. "Not as I will, but as you will" is the essence of holiness.

In fact the two halves always include each other. We pray or contemplate because it is our duty, it is the *act* God wills for us. And we act in doing our daily duty because we are being *receptive* to God's will.

Each involves the other. To *act* according to God's will is, first, to *surrender* to it. And if we surrender to it, we *will* act, for it is His will for us to act. What Mary told the servants who had run out of wine at the wedding feast at Cana, "Do whatever he tells you" (Jn 2:5), she tells us, too. The "do" means activity, and the "whatever he tells you" means receptivity. They are two dimensions of the same act. They do not alternate, though consciously focusing on our external activity and consciously focusing on inner contemplation in prayer do alternate. The Benedictine motto "ora et labora" ("pray and work") means both (1) that life is rightly divided into times for external, physical work and times for internal, spiritual prayer, since God wills both for us, and also (2) that prayer is itself a work and work should itself be a form of prayer.

Ignoring the outer world and action would be irresponsible. "Obedience to the clearly expressed and definite will of God . . . implies normal vigilance, care, prudence, and discretion" (p. 77). Receptivity to His supernatural will demands natural activity; our supernatural duty demands faithfulness to our natural duties; and supernatural faith demands using our natural reason.

This last example of activity and receptivity together, the relation between faith and reason, means three things: (1) that it is the receptivity of trusting *faith* that demands our use of our reason and our action, (2) that what this trusting faith demands is *active reason*, and (3) that this trusting faith *demands* active reason.

~

A theological footnote about activity and receptivity: in the Christian theology of the Trinity there is receptivity even in God, for the Son is begotten by the Father as well as the Father begetting the Son, and both are equally divine acts as well as equally Divine Persons.

Also, the Son receives and obeys the Father's will. He says He comes to do not His own will but the Father's will. Yet He is equal to the Father. This shows, at the highest level, that receptivity is not an imperfection, except accidentally, because of time, when the received effect is dependent on the prior acting cause. But in themselves, the essences of giver and receiver are equally valuable.

This is the metaphysical basis for women's equality (but not sameness) with men. A woman's receptivity is the power and the glory of her inner being; it is not a shameful relegation to secondary status by a male chauvinist society.

28

Spiritual Warfare

Christianity is full of paradoxes: God is both one being, substance, essence, or nature and three Persons; Christ is both fully human and fully divine; we are both free and predestined; God is both perfectly just and perfectly merciful; the Christian life is both active and receptive—and it is also both peaceful and warlike.

De Caussade writes; "O Lord, may you rule my heart . . . and let it triumph over all its enemies" (p. 50).

We have enemies. The word is used hundreds of times in Scripture, especially in the Psalms, Scripture's prayer book for everyone. For life is spiritual warfare for everyone. There can be no spiritual pacifists. The Devil and his evil spirits really exist and hate us and want to destroy our souls. If that is not true, then Jesus, the Church, the Bible, and all the saints are deluded, obsessed, and insane, because they not only believe that, they live it.

Life is war. It is also true that life is peace and joy and love. The paradox cannot be resolved by dividing life into two compartments, the loving and the warring, because love itself is war. Love wars. Love fights. Love even *hates* its enemies, which are not flesh and blood but the enemies and perversions of love, especially greed and lust and pride, and refusals to love, especially indifference and

sloth and selfishness. Love no more can tolerate these enemies than light can tolerate darkness. Whenever the two
meet, there is war, and one of them destroys the other.

As de Caussade says, it is our very heart, the very center of our souls, our very identities, that have enemies.
That is why we must let God rule our hearts: not only
because that is true and right and just and sane and in conformity with reality (that too, of course, and that first of
all) but also because that is the only possible way our
hearts can ever triumph over all the little spies that are
the poisonous seeds that Satan has planted in the good
earth of our hearts. Those little spies are called sins.

Love and hate, and peace and war, are not only com-
patible but necessitate each other when they each have
their proper objects. For the more we love God and His
children, including ourselves, the more we hate the sins
that are destroying their happiness and their hope. Love
and hate are incompatible only when the objects of love
or hate are misidentified as real concrete beings: you can't
both love and hate God or His children, and you can't
both love and hate the sins that war against them. Insofar
as we do, we have divided hearts. But at the center of
this center (the heart), we must identify with one or the
other, darkness or light, sin or sanctity.

Just as the peace of God is not the illusory peace that
the world gives, so the spiritual war that is part of holiness
is not the confused war that the world wages. The peace
of God is not peace with greed, lust, and pride, not peace
with the world, the flesh, and the devil, but it is peace
with neighbor, self, and God. And the war of God is not
war with neighbor, self, or God but war with greed, lust,

and pride, with the world, the flesh, and the devil. The two wars are at war with each other, and so are the two peaces.

29

Grace

Grace is another name for love, undeserved love. Grace is God's activity, and as de Caussade says "Only God's activity can make us holy" (p. 54). And therefore our job is not to produce it but to receive it. Whatever is received, is received according to the nature of the receiver, says the wise maxim of the philosophers. Water takes the shape of the bucket into which it is poured, and so does grace. It looks Petrine in Peter, Marian in Mary, and Johannine in John.

Those buckets into which God's grace is received are our souls. And all human souls have free will, by their own essential nature. So when God's grace enters a human soul, it does not set aside that soul's free will but perfects it. Grace turns free will on, not off. And therefore we must freely choose to receive God's grace. For grace is a gift (we do not deserve it: that's why it's called grace rather than justice), and a gift must be not only freely given but also freely received. A blow on the head or a bullet in the heart is not a gift.

It's not that God does His half of the contract, putting His money on the table, and then waits to see whether we will do our half. Grace and free will are not a fifty-fifty deal but a one hundred-one hundred deal, like marriage.

It's God's grace that actualizes ("turns on") our very acceptance of it and also actualized our prior asking for it. Pascal, following Saint Augustine, has God saying to the soul, "Take comfort: you would not be searching for me unless you had already found me" (*Pensées* 553).

But this truth, the primacy of God's grace, should be learned after, not before, we seek Him. There is an order here. In our experience, our seeking comes first, and then our finding Him. But in God's experience, His seeking us comes first. We do not have God's experience, only our own; but He has revealed His experience to us, and that is why we know that His grace preceded even our seeking of Him. So the truth of the absolute primacy of God's grace should not be misused as fatalism and as an excuse for not seeking Him ("I guess God just didn't give me the grace to be interested enough to seek Him"), because that is to confuse our experience with God's. Its proper use and place is afterward—as in the hymn, "I sought the Lord *and afterward I knew* / He moved my soul to seek Him, seeking me. / It was I that found, O Savior true; / No, I was found by Thee."

The practical point for us is that we must (1) first actively seek God and His grace, not just passively sit around waiting for it to drop like a meteorite; (2) then choose to receive it in total abandonment (faith and hope); and (3) then thank Him for it and for starting the process and, therefore, for the whole process, including our two free choices, the choices to seek it actively and to abandon ourselves to receiving it. But there is a right order: we are to thank Him for it, and for our two previous free choices (to seek it and to accept it) *after* it has been done.

All three acts are ours and are free, and we can refuse them, and we are responsible for these choices; *and* all three acts are initiated by God's grace.

Of course it is never finally "done", that is, finished, in this life, so we must keep going back to step (1) and (2) again and again, even after step (3).

How do we do these three things? We just do it! There is no technology for it. It is too great for that. It is love. Technology is cause and effect; and the cause must be equal to or greater than the effect; and there is nothing greater to or equal to love; and therefore nothing can cause love but love.

30

Detachment

"Detachment" from everything but God means that God alone is enough. God is not alone, but God alone is enough.

He is not alone because He is a Trinity of Persons in love. And because He is love, He has given being to others, the creatures that He created, especially the only creatures that can freely love Him back, created persons, human or angelic.

God alone is enough because if God alone is not enough, then God is not God. If He *is* enough, well, then, He is enough. Then, as Saint Teresa said, "God alone suffices."

De Caussade says the same thing: "He is the all-perfect being, and when we possess him we need nothing else" (p. 29).

C.S. Lewis, referring to Saint Augustine, says, "He who has God and everything else has no more than he who has God alone" (*The Weight of Glory*).

But don't we need each other, too? "People who need people. . . ."

Saint Thomas Aquinas asks, in the *Summa*, whether the fellowship of human friendship is necessary for complete happiness in Heaven, and his answer sounds shocking at first. He says that although it certainly is necessary for complete happiness in this life, it is not in the next. For if God alone is not enough to satisfy all the desires and needs of our heart, then God is not God.

He then adds that the fellowship of friends, the "communion of saints", will in fact be present and perfected in the next life. But not because without it God alone is not enough, but because God is generous and gives more, not less, than what is enough. God alone is enough, but God is not alone.

Saint Anselm puts the point powerfully:

> One thing is necessary (Lk 10:42) This [God] is . . . that one thing necessary in which is every good. . . . For if particular goods are enjoyable, consider carefully how enjoyable is that good which contains the joyfulness of all goods. . . . Why, then, do you wander about so much, O insignificant man, seeking the goods of your soul and body? Love the one good in which all good things are, and that is sufficient. . . . For what do you love, O my flesh, what do you desire, O my soul? There it is, there it is, whatever you love, whatever you desire.
>
> If beauty delights you, "the just will shine as the sun" (Matt. 13:43).
>
> If the swiftness or strength or freedom of the body that nothing can withstand [delights you], "they will be like the angels of God" (Matt. 22:30), for it is "sown as a natural body and shall rise as a spiritual body" (1 Cor. 15:44) by a supernatural power.
>
> If it is a long and healthy life, a healthy eternity and an eternal health is there since "the just will live forever" (Wis. 5:16). . . .
>
> If it is satisfaction, they will be satisfied "when the glory of God will appear" (Ps. 16:15).

If it is quenching of thirst, "they will be inebriated with the abundance of the house of God" (Ps. 35:9).

If it is melody, there the choirs of angels play unceasingly to God.

If it is pleasure of any kind, not impure but pure, God "will make them drink from the torrent of His pleasure" (Ps. 35:9).

If it is wisdom, the very Wisdom of God will show itself to them.

If it is friendship, they will love God more than themselves and one another as themselves, and God will love them more than they love themselves. . . .

If it is peace, for all of them there will be one will, since they will have none save the will of God.

If it is power, they will be all-powerful with regard to their wills, as God is with His. For just as God will be able to do what He wills through Himself, so through Him they will be able to do what they will; because just as they will not will anything save what He wills, so He will will whatever they will, and what He intends to will cannot not be.

If it is honours and riches, God will set His good and faithful servants over many things (Matt. 25:21, 23); indeed, they will be called "sons of God" and "gods" (Matt. 5:9), and will in fact be so; and where the Son will be there also they will be, "heirs indeed of God and co-heirs with Christ" (Rom. 8:17).

If it is real security, they will indeed be as assured that this . . . good will never in any way fail them, as they will be assured that they will not lose it of their own accord, nor that the loving God will take it away against their will from those who love Him, nor that anything more powerful than God will separate God and them against their will. . . . [Rom 8:28–39—read it! Now!]

Ask your heart whether it could comprehend its joy in its so great blessedness? But surely if someone else whom you loved in every respect as yourself possessed that same blessedness, your joy would be doubled for you would rejoice as much for him as for yourself. If, then, two or three or many more possessed it you would rejoice just as much for each one as for yourself, if you loved each one as yourself. Therefore in that perfect and pure love of the countless holy angels and holy men where no one will love another less than himself, each will rejoice for every other as for himself. If, then, the heart of man will scarcely be able to comprehend the joy that will belong to it from so great a good, how will it comprehend so many and such great joys? Indeed, to the degree that each one loves some other, so he will rejoice in the good of that other; therefore, just as each one in that perfect happiness will love God incomparably more than himself and all others with him, so he will rejoice immeasurably more over the happiness of God than over his own happiness and that of all the others with him. But if they love God with their whole heart, their whole mind, their whole soul, while yet their whole heart, their whole mind, and their whole soul, is not equal to the grandeur of this love, they will assuredly so rejoice with their whole heart, their whole mind, and their whole soul, that their whole heart, their whole mind, and their whole soul will not be equal to the fullness of their joy.[1]

⁓

---

[1] Anselm of Canterbury, *Proslogion*, in *The Major Works* (Oxford: Oxford Univ. Press, 1998), chaps. 23-25.

We can and should anticipate this Heavenly vision to some extent in this life. For if we do not, if we do not believe this, if we believe that there is something besides God that is absolutely necessary to our happiness, then we are in idolatry and a state of addiction to it (all idols are addictions; God alone frees us). We are treating it as God. Worse, we are saying to God: "You are not enough. I won't accept Your offer to go to Heaven if You won't let me take my teddy bear with me. I love my teddy bear more than You. You are just a means to getting my teddy bear."

"Detachment" from the good things of this life is one of the hardest aspects of holiness. We all frequently violate "the great and first commandment" (Mt 22:38) and demand many other things besides God, because deep down we do not wholly believe that God alone is enough, even though we want to believe that. So we should all frequently pray, "I believe; help my unbelief!" (Mk 9:24). When we do fully believe it, this vision of God as all-sufficient makes detachment easy, even a joy, a kind of game. We are happy to give our toys away when we become adults and realize that they are only toys.

And the fact that nothing matters except God does not mean that nothing else matters. It means that they matter *because of God*, because their goods are all participations in God's goodness. And that means that they matter more, not less. They are only finite, but if the infinitely good will of the infinitely good God wills them for us, then they participate in infinity, in the true way, as gifts, rather than in the false way of idolatry. They are not gods, they do not suffice, but they are gifts of the One God who does suffice.

If Saint Teresa is wrong when she says that "God alone suffices", then something else is needed that God does not have, and in that case God is only *a* god, one of many. Then our god is too small, and we are polytheists, and our soul is split. Polytheism is schizophrenia, split personality. To be one person, we must love one Person.

That is why marriage (which is faithful, exclusive, indissoluble, and fruitful no matter how much we may try to redesign it or recreate it or change it) is God's primary training for Heaven.

31

Creation

The practical point of the all-sufficiency of God follows from the theological truth of creation.

God created us out of nothing. He may have evolved our bodies out of dust or clay or apes; but just as He created the whole material universe out of nothing, He created each soul out of nothing. That is why each soul is new in its unique substance or essence. It is not merely a new accidental, external shape that the same old matter took when a sperm and an ovum joined.

But if we are created out of nothing, if we did not create ourselves or each other (though we do *pro*create each other, as God's instrumental causes—that is why sex is holy), then of ourselves we are nothing. For each thing, of itself, if left untended, tends to fall back into that out of which it was made; and we were made out of nothing. Unless God said "Be!" to us at every moment, we would cease to be. The same is true of the universe as a whole. Everything sinks back to what it was made from unless it is continually provided for. Grey wood painted white gradually becomes grey if not repainted. That, says Chesterton, is the only argument against mere conservatism: to conserve something, you have to have an ongoing revolution to preserve it.

So our very existence is not our own: God is holding us in existence at every moment, at this moment. He is saying to us "Be!" just as He did at the moment of our conception. He's holding the whole world in His hands now, at this present moment.

Our Father in Heaven is not a deadbeat dad who leaves his children after bringing them into existence. God does not first work, then sleep (Jn 5:17). No one else can hold things in existence, any more than anyone else can give things existence, that is, create. God's command to "be!" echoes from the single Now of eternity into every now-moment of time. That is why every moment is holy: because it is filled with the presence and will and activity of God, at its very center, its very existence.

(For more on creation and existence, see appendix 1.)

32

God and You Only?

Augustine in his *Soliloquies*, imagines God asking him what he wants to know, and his reply is: "God and the soul." "Nothing more?" asks God. "Nothing whatever", says Augustine.

This does not exclude other people and the world; it relativizes them. For there is only one objective absolute, God; and there is only one subjective absolute, yourself. You can never be anyone but yourself, and God can never be anything but God. The whole question of life is the relation between these two absolutes. ("Religion" means, literally, "yoking or binding relationship".)

There are only two persons you can never, ever escape, not for one moment, either in time or in eternity: God and yourself.

Everything else is relative to these two. Everything else is a truck on the highway that stretches between yourself and God, as Jacob's Ladder stretched between Heaven and earth. All traffic, all life, all history is on that ladder, that highway.

That is why de Caussade is wise and realistic, not foolish and idealistic, when he says that all we need to do is to "Do [your] obvious duty as if nothing in the world existed except God and [you]" (p. 76). In other words, the key to holiness is, as Brother Lawrence said, simply to "practice the presence of God." Do everything under the eye of God, that is, under the eye of Absolute, Uncompromising Truth and Love.

33

Praying while Working

Very few people are good at doing two or more things at once, especially contemplating and acting, praying and working, Mary-ing and Martha-ing at the same time. But de Caussade shows you how to do just that, to unite Mary and Martha, to do the works of Martha in the spirit of Mary.

He does that by focusing on the same single motive for both: freely willing God's will. When God interrupts your action and wills you to pray or contemplate, even virtuous acting becomes a vice. When God interrupts your prayer and wills you to act, praying instead of acting becomes disobedience, even if that praying reached the highest levels of mystical prayer. I think it was Saint Francis who told his monks something like this: If you are rapt in ecstasy in contemplative prayer, and a hungry beggar knocks at the door, you must immediately (important word!) leave your ecstasy and open the door to him, because God has left your ecstasy and has entered that beggar, and you must do the same; you must go where God is.

When you change your acts, your heart does not have to change, because it can remain fixed on God's will. If you refuse to change your acts when God wills it, your heart changes, because it refuses God's will. There is one unchanging reality: God's will. There is also a changing reality: your will and your acts. If your heart chooses to adhere to Him, then it remains at peace amid all life's changes because all life's changes are only the various forms taken by the one unchanging, absolute reality: God and His will, the one unchanging love of your heart.

In *The Practice of the Presence of God*, Brother Lawrence confessed that he hated kitchen cleanup work (he was a guy!), but he had the same peace and presence of God there as in the chapel. If only our will is single and wills just one absolute, God—His truth and His goodness—we will find His presence and providence and peace everywhere.

Our deepest problem is not that we are too relativistic but that we are not relativistic enough. God is the only absolute; everything else is relative to Him and His will. We are idolaters when we absolutize something else—anything else—other than that. That is always the ultimate reason why we are confused and unhappy.

We are also too relativistic, when we relativize God's will so that we can absolutize our own. Wrong relativism and wrong absolutism are aspects of the same thing: idolatry. And right relativism (of our stuff) and right absolutism (of God's stuff) also are aspects of the same thing: sanctity and sanity.

Once we are attached to the one absolute (God's will), we can be relativistic about everything else, including whether to pray or work. The answer to this and all other questions is: "Do whatever he tells you" (Jn 2:5).

34

Gratitude

Even the smallest hint of this vision (the thirty-three chapters above) elicits only one reasonable, sane response: gratitude.

Gratitude is the first spontaneous beginning of religion. One of my teachers, who was also one of the wisest men I ever met, Father W. Norris Clarke, S.J., told me that he once went to Tibet, on his own, just to see how Buddhist monks lived the life of holiness. He was welcomed by the abbot, and they had deep, mutually respectful, and profitable conversations. Before Father Clarke left, the abbot said: "Our religions are very different, but I think our hearts are not so different. I would like to test that idea, if you agree. Let us each answer the same question and compare our answers. My question is: What is the single most essential attitude of the human heart that is necessary for any and all religion? I will also ask this question to three of my monks. I have never asked them this question before, so they will have to answer from their own hearts. Let us write our answers on five pieces of paper and then unfold them and read them aloud." Father Clarke agreed that was an excellent experiment. When the five slips of paper were unfolded, the same word appeared on all five: "gratitude".

Father Clarke then said to the abbot, "That is very impressive, and very enlightening. What do you mean by gratitude. Gratitude for what?" The reply was: "For everything. For matter, for mind, for life, for death, for everything that has existence, for the mystery of existence itself." Father Clarke again thought that impressive and profound. Then he asked, "You Buddhists do not believe in a Creator-God, so when you are grateful for everything, to whom are you grateful?" The abbot's honest reply was: "We do not know the answer to that question." It was Father Clarke's turn to smile: "Well, we do."

The worst moment in the life of an atheist is the moment when he feels this deep, cosmic gratitude and knows, deep down, that it is very right to feel it, and there is no one to be grateful to. It is like Romeo feeling profound romantic love in a world where there is no Juliet.

～

We express our gratitude especially in three ways: prayer, fasting, and almsgiving. For we express gratitude in both words and deeds, and prayer is the words while fasting and almsgiving are the two sides of the deeds. Fasting means, not just fasting from food, but sacrificing anything to which our hearts are attached for the sake of God and others. Almsgiving is the positive side of fasting: it means, not just giving money, but giving whatever we have to others. Those are the deeds of gratitude, which are the deeds of love. The words of gratitude are prayer, especially the prayer of praise.

Our prayers are radically inadequate. Therefore God has provided for us many things to make up for that inadequacy. The Scriptures are one of them, especially the prayers in the Psalms. The Church's public liturgy is another. Others' prayers help, too. So do the "charisms" ("gifts") of prayer, including the charismatic gift of tongues.

This is a gift that is meant for the whole Church (according to the New Testament: see 1 Cor 14:5) but is often associated with only a "fringe" of it. One form of this gift is speaking in earthly languages you have never learned. That was what happened on Pentecost, and it was striking and miraculous. It still occurs occasionally, but rarely. The much more common form is the gift of a prayer language you do not understand, and neither does anyone else but God. God gives this gift because rational understanding can get in the way. That psychological principle is behind repetitions in all religions, such as the word "Om" or mantras in Hinduism and, in Western religions, repetitions in the public liturgy and in private devotions like the rosary and the chaplet of divine mercy. As a busy mother gives a toddler a toy to distract him, the heart gives the intellect and its tongue the toy of words to distract it so that the heart can do its work of mysterious love, the love that goes beyond the mind, undistracted and unhindered by the intellect.

Since this is a gift for all, we should all ask God for it and use it when it is given. Then we will be able to express our gratitude and praise in words that do not have conceptual frames, borders, and limits, words whose meanings are known to God alone, words that are God's own language.

For our gratitude to God for His infinite and incomprehensible beauty and for His even more incomprehensible love can never be expressed in words. For words have limits; the concepts they express are meaningful to us only because they are like little pictures with big frames or rivers with banks or lakes with shores. Praying in tongues is one way of removing the banks from the rivers so that the rivers become the sea.

35

"Progressive" or "Conservative"?

Is this vision of life progressive or conservative? Both and neither.

John Beevers, the translator of *Abandonment*, says about its teaching that it "has nothing new about it. How could it? Caussade was a Christian" (pp. 14–15).

A Christian is not an innovator. Christ is the innovator. A Christian is a disciple.

Yet, on the other hand, Christ was not an innovator. He summarized his whole life in these two sayings: (1) "My teaching is not mine, but his who sent me" (Jn 7:16) and (2) "I seek not my own will but the will of him who sent me" (Jn 5:30).

The apparent contradiction is easily explained. In relation to all other men, Christ was the supreme innovator. In relation to his Father, he was the supreme conformist. And the second fact is the whole reason for the first one.

All the truly Christian spiritual masters, all the saints, all the faithful, orthodox theologians, say the same thing about how to be holy. (This book is not at all original.) For that thing is simply Christ's thing. That is enough. That is more than enough. That is infinitely more than enough.

The objection then arises that this way of life is "conservative", "old-fashioned", "hide-bound", "traditionalistic", and "outdated".

On the contrary, there is nothing more radically new, creative, and unpredictable than what comes from this "conservatism" of abandonment to God's will. Look what came of it in the case of Christ!

Here is how de Caussade answers the objection that this way of life is pinned to one age alone, an age of religion that has now passed into the past. (This "modernist" objection, this "chronological snobbery", as C. S. Lewis calls it [in *Surprised by Joy*], was already in the air in de Caussade's "progressive", "enlightened" age.) "In every age, including this one, God's will works through every moment. . . . Can we imagine that in the days of old there was a secret method of abandoning oneself to the divine will that is now out of date?" (p. 48).

This refutes both traditionalism and progressivism. Traditionalism holds that it is now out of date because the present is worse than the past, which we have lost and left behind, like a beautiful town through which our train has passed and to which it cannot turn back, alas! Progressivism holds that it is now out of date because the present is better than the past, which we have lost and left behind like an ugly slum through which our train has passed and to which it cannot turn back, hurrah! "The sacrament of the present moment" refutes both the traditionalist's obsession with the past and the progressivist's obsession with the future.

For the present moment is neither the past nor the future. Conservatives must learn to stop looking to the past, and progressives must learn to stop looking to the future. These are two of mankind's hardest temptations to resist. Satan always wants us to live in unreality rather than reality, and these are two effective ways of doing it; for only the present is real. Remember how impossible it was to try to twist and turn yourself out of the present? You literally can't live in the past or the future; all you can do is forget that you are living in the present and think you are living in the past or the future or wish you were living in the past or the future. But when you do that, you can only do that in the present.

So let's begin. There isn't much time left. We have to rehearse, to practice here what we will be doing there forever. It is like a dance, and we are clumsy and tempted to give up. But God will never let us go until we do it perfectly, for He will never let us go until we have the joy for which we were created, and we will never have that joy until we do the dance.

A Meditation on the Relationship between *Being* and God's Will

(Warning: metaphysics ahead. Not for everybody's taste. Go on to appendix 2 if you have allergies to abstractions.)

What is the supreme perfection in God?

Love, you say. Fine, but if that love does not *exist*, it is not a *real* perfection. Nothing has any real value unless it is real. And to be real means to exist.

So the first or final perfection is the act of existing, which is what is meant by being itself. Nothing else is really real unless it exists. A million merely-thought-up dollars or merely-possible dollars or potential dollars or the *essence of* a million dollars is not as perfect as one real dollar, one dollar that actually exists.

~

Everything else exists only because God commanded it to be. God commands all things that are with one word: "Be!" Only He can make things be, only He can make something out of nothing, only He can create. You can't give what you don't have, and only God is being by nature, by His essence; therefore, only God can give being.

And that is what creating means: to give being to something that did not have it, to make something out of nothing. Only God can create.

When He created the universe, He created all matter and energy and all time and space, all that has being outside Himself, in one act. For He is not in time, and therefore He does not do one thing after another in time, though we who are in time receive one thing after another because one of the things He makes is time itself.

So when He said "Be", He said it to everything that is, was, or will be. When He said "Let there be light", He saw everything in that light, including the buzzing swarm of flies around His beloved Son's sacred head on the Cross and the apparent triumph of those flies and of Satan (one of whose names, "Beelzebub", means "the lord of the flies").

~

What did God mean when He said "Be!"? What is it to be?

It is to exist.

To say that being means the act of existing sounds like the most abstract of all concepts, but it is exactly the opposite. It is hard (in fact impossible) to conceive, not because it is too abstract, but because it is not abstract at all. It is not merely the *fact* that something exists (that's abstract), but the *act* of its existing. That's concrete. "Concrete" does not mean "cement". In fact, "cement" is abstract: it is a *kind* of thing, not a thing. In philosophical language, it is a nature, not a substance. Saint Michael the

Archangel is concrete; cement is abstract. The nature of an angel is abstract, as the nature of concrete is abstract, while a particular real concrete building is concrete, as a particular angel, like Saint Michael, is concrete. Every human being is concrete; humanity is abstract. That is why we are never told to love humanity but only our neighbors, one by one.

So the act of existing, which sounds abstract, is not. It is individuated. It is always the act of existing of this individual thing or person.

Concepts are abstract. Whatever can be put into a concept is abstract, and whatever is abstract can be put into a concept. Since existence (that is, the act of existing) is not abstract, it cannot be put into a concept. We have no concept of existing. We express it in judgments, not concepts: God exists; Michael exists; Mars exists.

So existence is not a concept. It is an act, not a fact. It is the active energy to stand outside nothingness, the moxie, the chutzpah, to BE. Things are given being by the only one whose name is Being, who says, not "I am Zeus" or "I am Ahura Mazda", but "I AM WHO AM." Only the God whose essence is existence can give existence to anything else.

God's essence is existence. God is unlimited existence. Everything else HAS existence; God IS existence.

Only God creates (gives existence) because you can't give what you don't have, the effect cannot exceed its cause. Since God's essence is existence, His existence needs no other cause; everything else's essence has to be given existence by an external cause, a cause outside its essence.

The act of existence is the supreme actuality, the supreme perfection. Even after all other perfections are thought of, as essences, as things that *can* exist, things that are possible, the question remains: *Do* they exist, are they actual? Add spirit to matter, intellect to spirit, infallibility to intellect, omniscience to infallibility, and all you are doing is adding more perfections with each addition. But is such a being, a being with these attributes, real? You must add the act of existing to all perfections, and only then are ANY of them real rather than only concepts, actual rather than only possible.

Because God is existence itself, unlimited existence, existence not limited by any essence, He is not definable or conceivable. And that is why all the mystics, of every religion in the world, who catch a glimpse of this ultimate perfection say the same thing: that it cannot be put into words or concepts. It surpasses human thought.

Wittgenstein says: "It is not how things are in the world that is mystical but that it exists."

Heidegger says that "the fundamental question of metaphysics" is "why is there anything at all rather than nothing?" The fundamental question is not, as Plato thought, "what" a thing is (every Platonic dialogue is about that, about an essence, a definition, a concept, such as justice or piety or learning) but why it exists, why anything exists. Plato never asked that ultimate question.

And the answer is God.

Now let us compare the act of existing with the *will* of God and so move from philosophical theology to practical spirituality and holiness. (They are connected.)

The will of God is always concrete, just as an act of a human being's will is concrete. It is real, it exists, it happens. So since both the will of God and existence are concrete, not abstract, they could match. The abstract and the concrete cannot match.

God alone has the power to create. He made an image of His power to create when He gave us free will; for only when we will a choice does that choice exist. We cannot create matter, but we can create choices. We can create choices to trust, to believe, to hope, to love, or to refuse to.

It is a terrifying power. It alone accounts for the existence of Hell. The loving God sends no one to Hell against his will. He does not push us or tempt us into the abyss. Satan tempts us but cannot push us. We ourselves jump. No one knows how many jump, but even one is enough for an ultimate tragedy that is literally incomparable.

But this terrifying power of free choice, without which there could be no Hell, is also something without which there could be no Heaven. A Heaven we did not freely choose, a Heaven that was forced on us, would not be a Heaven. It would be a prison.

Heaven is the will of God. Willing God's will is not merely the *cause* of Heaven, it is the very life of Heaven.

To align our will with God's will is to align ourselves with reality, with being, for God's will is being. His Ten Commandments are ten ways of being real rather than unreal. All ten can be summarized in one word: "Be!" Christ's Beatitudes are "be attitudes".

That is why we must be holy. To be holy is to be, for to be holy is to be like God ("Be holy for I [the Lord your God] am holy"), and God is being. To be holy is to be, and to be unholy is to un-be.

So Be.

APPENDIX TWO

A Dialogue between Stupid and Sensible (the Two Parts of My Soul)

STUPID: I know some people can become saints, but I'm not one of them. The gap between me and the saints is like the gap between a pebble and a mountain.

SENSIBLE: I have four answers to that. First, a pebble is a part of a mountain. It's made of the same stuff. Second, all the saints started where you are, as pebbles. Third, you're not a pebble—no one is—but a seed. You're small, but alive. Your whole identity is to grow. Fourth, you *will* become a saint because everyone in Heaven is a saint. God will not let you go until you are. It's unavoidable. In fact, I think you know that. That's why you're reading this book. So stop the false humility.

STUPID: It's not false humility, it's honesty. I'm a really stupid, selfish, silly sinner.

SENSIBLE: Of course you are. Everyone is. That's what Original Sin means. That's the real equality. We all start at zero. And that's why you have to change: you have a long road ahead.

STUPID: The road is too long.

SENSIBLE: But there is no other road to Heaven.

STUPID: I'll make it to Heaven, I'll just take a long time to get there, through Purgatory. I've got some faith and hope and charity (a little, anyway), so I'm not going to Hell.

SENSIBLE: But is that all you care about? Is that what your faith is to you: an eternal fire insurance policy?

STUPID: What should it be?

SENSIBLE: A marriage to God. To God! How dare you be content with the minimum?

STUPID: I told you: I'm very stupid.

SENSIBLE: But He will never be content with that. And He's the boss, not you.

STUPID: You're asking for a radical change. You're asking too much.

SENSIBLE: No, He's asking that. Are you His judge, His critic?

STUPID: I'm afraid.

SENSIBLE: Of what?

STUPID: It costs too much.

SENSIBLE: But the alternative costs more.

STUPID: Hell, you mean?

SENSIBLE: No, I was just thinking of life on earth without this total abandonment. A half life, always torn between yourself and God, never wholly either one. Drawing limits, keeping a little bit, out of fear. That will drive you crazy. Give it all up, and you will be free!

STUPID: I know I will, but I can't.

SENSIBLE: Yes, you can. You know you can; that's why you feel guilty for not doing it. If you really believed you couldn't do it, you would feel no guilt. You feel no guilt about not being Superman and flying over tall buildings, do you?

STUPID: I do feel guilt for my lukewarmness. And I know the saints are happier than I am. I even know from experience that whenever I do give God everything, for just a few moments, and stop holding onto things, I have real joy and peace; and when I don't, I don't. But it doesn't last. I'm afraid I'm an addict, a selfaholic.

SENSIBLE: Welcome to the human race. And welcome to God's rehab program. He's a realist, you know, as well as an idealist. He doesn't expect instant perfection.

STUPID: What does He expect that I'm not giving Him?

SENSIBLE: The refusal to give up, ever. Keep getting back on the horse every time you fall off.

STUPID: But I fall a million times a day.

SENSIBLE: Only a million? That's no obstacle to Him. He can count to infinity.

STUPID: He will forgive me then.

SENSIBLE: He will forgive you for anything and everything except not even trying, giving up for good, forever.

STUPID: That's what Hell is?

SENSIBLE: That's one road to Hell, despair of God's grace, God's love, God's forgiveness, and God's power to make you holy. The other road is pride, or presumption: not even asking for forgiveness.

STUPID: I don't think I'm on either of those two roads. But I'm not holy, either.

SENSIBLE: Wrong. There are only two roads, not three. The only alternative to Hell is Heaven.

STUPID: What about Purgatory?

SENSIBLE: That's Heaven's bathroom, where you wash up before dinner. That's the beginning of Heaven. It's not a compromise between Hell and Heaven. There can be no such compromise.

STUPID: But life is gradual, change is gradual, progress or regress is gradual.

SENSIBLE: Of course it is. But directions aren't. Up and Down are the only two directions.

STUPID: So is God demanding one great act of total renunciation and abandonment or a gradual progress?

SENSIBLE: Both. It's not an either/or. The first is the beginning of the second, as getting pregnant is the beginning of motherhood.

STUPID: So are you saying I'm on the road called despair if I don't do that first thing?

SENSIBLE: No, I'm saying you've already chosen that first thing. If you hadn't, you wouldn't be worried about it and seeking it and reading this book.

STUPID: If I've already done it, why do I have to do it again?

SENSIBLE: If you've already said "I do" to your wife, do you never have to say that again? You keep doing it, more and more, especially after you keep forgetting to do it.

STUPID: Actually, I think I may be in despair. Not of God's goodness, but of mine.

SENSIBLE: As I just said, if you were, you would not be reading this book.

STUPID: So I've already made that fateful choice to become a saint?

SENSIBLE: Do you *want* to do it?

STUPID: Yes.

SENSIBLE: Then you've done it.

STUPID: How do you know that?

SENSIBLE: Because it's the one thing you get just by wanting it. Because it IS a wanting.

STUPID: But I'm so weak. My want is weak, my will is weak.

SENSIBLE: Can there be a strong elephant if there's no elephant?

STUPID: No.

SENSIBLE: Can there be a weak elephant if there's no elephant?

STUPID: No.

SENSIBLE: Can there be a strong will if there's no will?

STUPID: No.

SENSIBLE: So can there be a weak will if there's no will?

STUPID: No.

SENSIBLE: So if you have a weak will to give yourself to God, a weak will to be holy, then you have a will to give yourself to God, you have a will to be holy.

STUPID: It's a divided will.

SENSIBLE: Same argument. A divided will is a will.

STUPID: I don't know. I don't feel it in me.

SENSIBLE: It's not a feeling. It's a willing.

STUPID: But it's so weak! Maybe it's *too* weak.

SENSIBLE: Of course it's too weak; that's why God wants to strengthen it.

STUPID: I mean too weak to get to Heaven.

SENSIBLE: It's too weak to *endure* Heaven, that's true. That's why God wants to strengthen it.

STUPID: Maybe it's too weak to do this "abandonment" thing.

SENSIBLE: Do you want to do it?

STUPID: Of course. That's why I'm reading this book.

SENSIBLE: Then you've done it.

STUPID: But so weakly!

SENSIBLE: Yes, but you're forgetting the all-important thing. You're looking at yourself instead of looking at Him. Look at the One to whom you are so weakly abandoning yourself. How powerful He is! How dangerous! He's a terror, that one! Whenever you say "Thy will be done" to Him, you'd better duck. Actually, I mean exactly the opposite: *Don't* duck. Get ready to catch His pitch. Because He will certainly throw some at you as soon as you tell Him that you are in His game instead of yours.

STUPID: I have no problem with His pitches: He's perfect, so they have to be perfect, too. But I have a real problem with my catches. I usually drop the ball.

SENSIBLE: Don't you think He knows that? He tailors His pitches to your weak ability to catch them.

STUPID: Then why does He pitch so many curve balls that I can't catch instead of easy lobs that I can?

SENSIBLE: He gives you plenty of easy lobs. More than you know. Everything you choose that's good, such as being honest with me right now, and even little things like smiling at me, are lobs from Him that you've caught. You're just much more aware of the pitches you drop.

STUPID: But there are plenty of those. Why does He throw me so many that I drop?

SENSIBLE: To show you how far you have to go on the road you're already on. To show you how high the mountain is that you are destined to climb. He will take you to the top. Just take it one step at a time, one little sacrifice at a time. Don't try to go faster than grace. His banquet isn't fast food.

STUPID: I'm also afraid some of His pitches will hurt me, so I shy back from them.

SENSIBLE: You mean you're afraid He'll ask you to suffer and to sacrifice.

STUPID: Yes. I'm a coward.

SENSIBLE: He sends you just the right sufferings to toughen you up. He knows what He's doing.

STUPID: How do they work?

SENSIBLE: When a fast ball hits you in the gut, you have no choice but to suffer. He makes you suffer against your will. So the good it does you doesn't depend on your weak and cowardly will. Some things do depend on your will; some things happen only if you freely will them; but as you say, you're weak, so if He limited His gifts to you to the ones that needed your free cooperation, you wouldn't have nearly as many gifts, as much grace, as you would if He also sent those fastballs into your gut over which you have no control.

STUPID: He's tricky.

SENSIBLE: Yes. He's like a wise doctor who sees that his patient is too weak for self-surgery, so he uses anesthesia. Death will be the final, total anesthesia, when you stop jumping all over His operating table, telling Him what not to do. Then you'll get that new heart you want. You've got to go under.

STUPID: I'm scared of being out of control.

SENSIBLE: But how terrible it would be for us if there were nothing that was out of our control anymore, if our technology made us into gods! That's the danger of technology. It's exactly the same danger as riches, which Jesus constantly warned against. Technology and riches are two forms of the same thing: power. That's why poor people are blessed and are often holier than rich ones.

STUPID: This love of His is a very tough love and a very mysterious one. It doesn't look like love.

SENSIBLE: That's because it doesn't look like our love. Our love can't be that tough because we don't have His wisdom; we can't see the future; we don't always know what's best for each other in the long run. That's why it's arrogant to play God and say "I know what you need. You need to suffer. So I'm going to supply your need." Because we don't know that. And God does.

STUPID: Don't we sometimes know that?

SENSIBLE: Yes, but rarely. Like punishing small, rebellious children, or criminals. That's when the gap between our wisdom and theirs is great. But it's never nearly as great as the gap between God's wisdom and ours.

STUPID: So His love doesn't look like ours because it's tougher.

SENSIBLE: Yes, but also tenderer! We can't combine toughness and tenderness as He can. That's why His love doesn't look like love: because it doesn't look like our love.

STUPID: How do you know so much about God's love?

SENSIBLE: Same way you do: look at Jesus. There you see both the toughness and the tenderness in perfect unity. Was anyone in history both tougher and tenderer?

STUPID: Is that why all those novels about Jesus are so embarrassingly bad?

SENSIBLE: Exactly! The real Jesus, the Jesus of the Gospels, is so different from anyone else who ever lived (and yet most deeply connected with everyone who ever lived!)

that He always surprises us. And fiction never surprises us, only fact surprises us, because our fiction only comes from us. The real Jesus is so much bigger than our best imagination that nobody can write good Jesus fiction.

STUPID: Wait a minute. You said at the beginning of your book that it was for everybody except atheists, not just for Christians; that it was religiously neutral or universal. Now you fall back on Jesus when I ask you how you know God.

SENSIBLE: I have to. He makes me do that.

STUPID: Why?

SENSIBLE: Because no other religious founder ever claimed to be God. If I accept that, then my answer to "Who is God?" has to be *there*. And if don't accept that, I'm not a Christian at all. In fact I have to say he's an imposter, an idiot, and probably insane.

STUPID: So only Christians can know God?

SENSIBLE: Not at all. Everyone can know God.

STUPID: How?

SENSIBLE: By honestly using their reason and moral conscience and by letting nature teach them.

STUPID: Then how can Jesus say that He is "the way and the truth and the life" and that no one can come to God the Father except through Him?

SENSIBLE: Because whenever anyone knows God, He's acting on them, He's the Mind of God.

STUPID: Non-Christians don't believe that.

SENSIBLE: Of course not. If they did, they'd become Christians. But it's true anyway.

STUPID: Believing something is true doesn't make it true.

SENSIBLE: Of course not. But believing something is false doesn't make it false, either.

STUPID: You have very clever answers, but that doesn't mean they're true.

SENSIBLE: Of course not. But you've just insulted me. Twice. "Clever" and "not true" are both insults. My answers are true without being clever, not clever without being true.

STUPID: That's a very clever answer.

SENSIBLE: But it's true.

STUPID: I'm sorry, I didn't mean to insult you. I guess I was just trying to avoid admitting that what you say is true, because if I did, I'd have no excuse for not doing it.

SENSIBLE: Yes, you were. We do that all the time. But that's the most sensible thing you've said yet.

STUPID: This God is really worth abandoning everything to!

SENSIBLE: And that's the other most sensible thing you've said yet. In fact, that's a key to becoming holy: look at Him a lot more and at yourself a lot less. The more you do that, the easier abandonment is.

STUPID: That's a really powerful psychological principle.

SENSIBLE: Yes, but even looking at the powerful psychological principle isn't as powerful as looking at Him.

STUPID: That's why we have to pray, right?

SENSIBLE: Exactly. And that's the third sensible thing you have said! We pray not just to get things from Him but to see Him, to look at Reality.

STUPID: Shouldn't we look at our own faults, too?

SENSIBLE: Briefly, yes, and then move on, after we admit them and accept His forgiveness. If we keep looking at ourselves, that's not humility, that's pride: Ooh, look at me, look at what a great sinner I am!

STUPID: So humility doesn't mean having a low opinion of yourself?

SENSIBLE: No, it means having no opinion of yourself, because you're looking at Him, instead.

STUPID: We can't see Him, of course.

SENSIBLE: Not with the eyes of the body. But we can see Him a little bit with the eyes of the soul, with reason and conscience. And we can see Him best with the eyes of the heart, which are faith and hope and love, especially love. The heart has eyes, you know. They see.

STUPID: "Seeing is believing", they say.

SENSIBLE: They have it backward. Believing is seeing. And so is loving.

STUPID: What's the best way to love Him?

SENSIBLE: He told us: love His kids, your neighbors.

STUPID: How?

SENSIBLE: He'll show you a hundred ways every day.